Effective Behaviour Management in the Primary Classroom

Effective Behaviour Management in the Primary Classroom

Fiona Shelton and Simon Brownhill

Open University Press
McGraw-Hill Education
McGraw-Hill House
Shoppenhangers Road
Maidenhead
Berkshire
England
SL6 2QL

email: enquiries@openup.co.uk
world wide web: www.openup.co.uk

and Two Penn Plaza, New York, NY 10121-2289, USA

First published 2008

A catalogue record of this book is available from the British Library

ISBN-13:   9780335225415 (pb) 9780335225408 (hb)
ISBN-10:   0335225411 (pb) 0335225403 (hb)

Library of Congress Cataloguing-in-Publication Data
CIP data applied for

Fictitious names of companies, products, people characters and/or data that may be used herein (in case studies or in examples) are not intended to represent any real individual, company, product or event.

Typeset by BookEns Ltd, Royston, Herts.
Printed in in the UK by Bell and Bain Ltd, Glasgow.

The *McGraw·Hill* Companies

Contents

To our families and friends

Acknowledgements

Thanks to Fiona Richman for being so patient and generous with time. We had a lot going on and wanted to give you the book you deserve – hope it lives up to it!

BB for your support and patience – thank you for cooking dinner for me and for giving me the time and space to write this book.

To the 'Badders Girls' – for all the missed badminton games!

To my family, for supporting me through my endeavours – always appreciated, much love to you all.

Fiona

I would like to sincerely thank the following people:

Fiona Richman for impressively remembering our first conversation at BERA in 2005 and being so understanding when OFSTED and a revalidation reared their ugly head at university!

Emily Bullock for kindly reading Chapter 6 – I hope that readers enjoy it as much as you said you did (and take note of the important aromatherapy consideration you suggested!).

My sister, Gemma, for feeding me information about the content of presentations delivered in schools by the police – cheers, Sugarfluff!

My brilliant parents – thank you for continuing to love me and support me in all I do – sorry for all the moaning!

My second family – thanks for still being there and being as supportive as ever.

My friends – I thank you for putting up with me and generally laughing at/with me!

Thank you all very much.

SPB

'A good teacher knows a word of praise can bring sunlight to the gloomiest of days.'

Pam Brown

1 What is your philosophy?

Introduction

Why another book on behaviour management? In an ever changing climate it is essential that we embrace changes linked to children, schools and systems. These changes, now more than ever, enable our pupils to move forward in their thinking and to contribute to society with a healthy and positive perspective of who they are. Whether you are studying at undergraduate level or working as a practising teacher, this book will offer an opportunity to develop critical thinking and analysis of practice in relation to theory. It will provide opportunities for you to evaluate and synthesize approaches and strategies to effective behaviour management.

Aims of this book

This book aims to support, extend and challenge thinking in a range of contexts in order to provide a wider perspective on pedagogy and practice within the educational field of behaviour management. It will explore principles which underpin a purposeful learning environment, practical strategies, techniques and approaches to maintain this, and analyse external factors that contribute to pupil behaviour. Behaviour management is a multi-faceted element of teaching and is not solely about children's behaviour; adults, including teachers, teaching assistants, parents and carers and those within the community, also play an essential role in the support and promotion of good forms of behaviour. This book will engage with philosophies, ideologies and practical suggestions in the management of behaviour in the current educational climate, both within and beyond the classroom setting.

A key principle of this book focuses upon the need for the reader to actively explore, understand and critically appraise why particular behaviours might occur and possible strategies to deal with these behaviours. The old adage 'prevention is better than cure' can certainly be attributed to behaviour management; therefore one of the rudiments of maintaining good behaviour is to ensure that there is sufficient scope for it to occur in the first place. We attempt to do this through analysing practice and engaging the reader actively in theoretical perspectives to maintain harmonious working relationships.

Who does this book target?

Whilst many of the key behaviour management texts are aimed at qualified teachers and professionals working in the primary setting, we felt that there was a real need to support the needs, abilities and experiences of those entering the teaching profession. This book provides accessible and engaging material at a suitable level to support trainees on their journey towards qualified teacher status (QTS). This does not mean that those working in the field of primary education are precluded from accessing the activities and tasks within the book. In fact we would encourage all teachers and support staff to analyse and develop their practice as part of their continuing professional development.

How will this book support you?

Those training to be qualified teachers may require more direction in developing their personal philosophy towards behaviour management, and thoroughly appreciating the complexities and difficulties of establishing and maintaining children's behaviour. Over the course of your training, you will be exposed to a wide range of approaches to behaviour management, some of which will be more positive than others. This book will allow you to critically reflect and analyse the practice you have seen and compare/contrast this to ideas and thinking to help formulate personal and professional development. For the qualified teacher and other teaching staff, this book will enable reflection and development of existing practice.

How is this book to be used?

Through the use of case studies, reflective tasks, familiar experiences and examples from the classroom this book aims to generate an interactive approach to the 'hows' and 'whys' of behaviour management. With its critical style of discussion, debate, reflection and analysis we hope to support and develop classroom practice to ease the stresses and strains of those entering the teaching profession and those already with experiences to maintain a purposeful working environment.

What you can you expect to find in the book?

Although it is impossible to compartmentalize behaviour management, we have divided the book into eight main chapters to enable you to focus specifically on a particular theme. It should be pointed out, however, that many elements of behaviour management can be easily transposed between chapters, and we would advocate this approach as you engage with the text. The focus of this initial chapter is the formulation of philosophies, exploring personal and professional contexts in which these will be studied.

Chapter 2 aims to put the practice into theory by exploring key theories and theorists, both established and contemporary, linked to a child's moral and social development.

Chapter 3 examines behaviour phases through the ages, dealing with typical behaviours that are manifested frequently in the primary classroom. Behaviours relating to educational needs and transitions between key stages form the basis for discussion. In Chapter 4 we examine how self-esteem, identity and emotional well-being directly impact on children's behaviour. This emotional intelligence also addresses an 'us' and 'them' perspective by analysing how our own personal attitudes, feelings and thoughts can influence the behaviour of the pupils we teach.

Putting policy into practice is at the heart of Chapter 5. This operates on three different levels. Firstly, the chapter examines a holistic approach to behaviour management through policy within the long term. Secondly, it discusses systems, schemes and classroom organization on a medium-term basis and, finally, a range of quick-fire strategies to engage pupils within the short term. Chapter 6 embraces creative approaches in the field of behaviour management, taking policy and practice 'outside the box'. Strategies linked to physical activity, multi-sensory approaches and peer/self management theories raise a deeper level of awareness to innovative practice. Challenging the creative approach concludes this chapter by developing a knowledge base for the twenty-first century.

Chapter 7 builds on this theme and enlists the use of the arts as a key resource to enable pupils to regulate their own behaviour. Through dance and music, we will provide a range of ideas that will engage pupils in thinking about the person they are and consequences of their words and actions. Story, drama and art also form key strands to enable pupils to make the right choices and investigate why people behave in particular ways.

Chapter 8 promotes the importance of behavioural partnerships. This studies how working with parents, carers and members of the wider community helps form a layered support mechanism in influencing the choices our young people make. We will explore a collaborative approach into how we can learn to work with others by initiating and sustaining involvement with multi-agency/integrated child services, businesses and community members. The book concludes with a summary of themes, ideas and messages for the way forward in terms of how you manage behaviour in your own classroom.

Explanation of the icons and interactive features of the text

To help you navigate your way through the text you will find a series of icons that alert you to particular features of the book, these include:

THINK Take a moment to contemplate an element of text, an idea or a strategy.

REFLECT This icon encourages you to critically analyse and relate ideas to your own practice.

CONSIDERATIONS There may be alternative approaches and thinking that you might like to incorporate into your own teaching strategies.

ACTIVITY This encourages you to engage with a practical task designed to support and further your understanding.

 NOTE There may be something here of which you may wish to take stock.

 QUESTIONS You might want to question the text or your own practice.

 SCENARIO Use these to apply strategies you know or have read about.

 TOP TIPS Quick-fire tips to help the day-to-day management of behaviour in your classroom.

 CASE STUDY Read and reflect on specific case studies to help you to further your understanding.

 EXTENDING YOUR LEARNING Engage with further reading or tasks to widen your knowledge, views and perspectives.

 STOP This icon indicates the need to take a moment to reflect critically on the topic of discussion.

 KEY POINTS

Whilst behaviour management is one of the key factors attributed to a successful school (OFSTED 2006) it is certainly not one of the easiest factors to develop without some trials and tribulations. This book is not designed in any way to be a 'quick fix' in terms of providing solutions, but is designed to encourage you to explore your own practice and develop your strategies for managing behaviour in the primary school setting.

Everyone who works with young people strives to ensure that they can achieve to the best of their ability and that this is not hindered by poor behaviour. The Every Child Matters agenda underpins this practice and encourages us to consider the emotional and social well-being of those we teach.

Every Child Matters – what is it?

Before we are able to consider personal philosophies with regard to behaviour management, it is important for us to contextualize current thinking and action in order to protect children. Let us consider some historical perspectives relating to this.

The Education Act of 1944 stipulated that parents were required to send their children to school unless they were being educated at home or by other means. Partnership working between parents and schools has always been an important feature of good practice and was highlighted in the Plowden Report (Central Advisory Council for Education 1967), which stressed the need for strong links between home and school.

REFLECT

How important do you think the Education Act (1944) and Plowden's Report (1967) are in the way children's behaviour is effectively managed by parents and teachers?

Prior to the Children's Act (1989), parents were deemed to have the rights to the protection and welfare of their children; with the introduction of the act the notion of 'parental rights' was removed and replaced with 'parental responsibility'. The Education Act (2004) disregarded previous views that children were passive in the choices in their lives and replaced this with the recommendation that children should be included in decisions about their own welfare. Following the death of Victoria Climbié, as reported by Lord Laming (2003), the Green Paper *Every Child Matters* (DfES 2003b) proposed integration of services in recognizing and meeting the holistic needs of children. By maintaining and improving relationships between health care and education, the Green Paper highlights five outcomes for children:

- being healthy;
- staying safe;
- enjoying and achieving;
- making a positive contribution;
- economic well-being.

For effective learning to take place children need to feel emotionally and physically secure in order to prevent poor health and disaffection having an adverse effect on their learning and lives.

> **THINK**
>
> • What do each of these outcomes mean in practice?
> • To which curriculum areas might they relate?
> • Who might be involved – which agencies and professionals?
>
> (For further information and support, refer to Chapter 8.)

Through the Every Child Matters agenda, extended schools are likely to provide an effective base for a range of services helping children to engage and achieve, and enabling stronger relationships with parents and carers in the community. This will be key for the five outcomes. Let us take a look at the five outcomes in greater detail.

> **ACTIVITY**
>
> Consult your copy of the Every Child Matters agenda (available from http://www.dfes.org.uk).
> Highlight key aspects of the detailed description of the five outcomes which you feel ready to embrace. Consider those for consultation with colleagues and those which require more research. Work to develop your knowledge and understanding of these by using websites, journal articles and DfES publications.

As a result of Every Child Matters, multidisciplinary and interprofessional working are more evident across Britain in a variety of settings. These include:

• children's centres;
• schools;
• extended schools, including social and health care;
• youth services;
• family learning.

Whilst most schools are moving towards integrating these services into their everyday practice, it is important to understand that this is not exclusive to Britain; for example, the No Child Left Behind Act of 2001 is a United States federal law that aims to improve the performance of primary and secondary schools by increasing the standards of accountability. Early Childhood Care for Development (ECCD) is a relatively new international approach focusing on the care that African children require in order to thrive. In their discussion of this approach Evans *et al.* (2000) explain that for a child to develop and learn in a healthy and normal way, it is important to meet the basic needs not only for protection, food and health care, but also for interaction and stimulation, affection, security, and learning through exploration and discovery.

> **ACTIVITY**
>
> How could these 'basic needs' become an integral feature of the curriculum you deliver to children in your class? Take a medium-term plan from one subject area of the curriculum you teach and critically reflect on the ways in which features of Every Child Matters embrace the basic needs of all children. Consider which needs are not addressed and what action is needed to fulfil the individual needs of every child.

Embracing Every Child Matters

Although Every Child Matters intends to meet the needs of all children, the agenda is particularly focused on those vulnerable in respect of their socio-economic background and day-to-day welfare. One way in which the agenda seeks to address these basic needs is through the well-being of the child. This should include emotional, social, academic and financial welfare in order to ensure that all children have access to the same rights and roles within the context in which they live. Schools are the 'hub' for this wrap-around care, providing education for young people and adults in addition to health and social guidance. These will include professionals such as:

- early years practitioners;
- teachers and teaching assistants;
- speech and language therapists;
- educational psychologists;
- social workers;
- adult educators;
- GPs and nurses;
- local authorities;
- police.

Of course this list is not exhaustive, and Chapter 8 deals with these partnerships in greater detail.

> **EXTENDING YOUR LEARNING**
>
> Using the internet, search three websites that will allow you to extend your understanding and knowledge of Every Child Matters and to explore further services and professionals that may be involved.

Let us take one outcome of the agenda, 'enjoying and achieving'. In the detailed description of the outcomes, the first strand is 'ready for school'. How might we consider how it may be put into practice in school?

Ready for school

First of all, what does this mean? Do we mean the physical interpretation – for example, is the child dressed appropriately? Have they had their breakfast? Have they got their lunch, homework, and so on? Have they had a wash? These are all basic needs that must be satisfied in order to thrive.

Or do we mean the emotional interpretation – can they socialize? Are they able to communicate with peers and other adults? Are they independent enough to be left for the day?

Or do we mean the academic interpretation – can they write their name? Do they recognize some words and numbers? Are they interested in books? Can they use imagination in their play?

How does 'ready for school' relate to the way in which children behave? Clearly, these aspects should be considered at the outset of dealing with behaviour management. This thinking informs your philosophy and practice and is likely to initiate a personal and professional audit of classroom beliefs.

Audit of practice and thinking

QUESTIONS

1. When you think of behaviour management what automatically comes to mind?
2. Why do you think this?
3. Can you think of five words you associate with behaviour management?
4. What behaviours have you recently encountered in your setting?
5. How did you respond to these behaviours?

How did you respond to the first question? Was your response positive or negative? A key characteristic of positive behaviour management stems from your own professional philosophy regarding behaviour management. Is behaviour management about your reaction, or is it about developing strategies to promote good behaviour? It is important for you to be clear about your response to this, as it will directly influence the kind of teacher you aspire to be.

CASE STUDY

Mr Jones and Mrs Simmons are both in their final year of their training and are on their final teaching placement in parallel classes. They are teaching numeracy to their respective classes of 36 Year 5 children. Mr Jones is half way through his main teaching exposition linked to handling data. A graph is shown on the interactive whiteboard.

Mr Jones:	What does this data tell us about our original question? Are the results as you expected?
Will:	Sir, I know!
Mr Jones:	Perhaps you do, Will, but we do not have shouting out in this class. Who else knows the answer? Thank you, Michael.
Will:	But sir, I know the answer! Please ask me!
Mr Jones:	No, Will. No shouting out. How many times do I have to say it? Go on Michael . . .
Will:	Oh come on! I know the answer! The graph shows that the most popular hobby in the class is playing computer games!
Mr Jones:	That's it! I told you once! I told you twice! Take the merits you earned this morning off your chart now. Go on, no arguments.
Will:	Fine, what's the point anyway?

Mrs Simmons is at the same stage in her lesson.

Mrs Simmons:	So, what does the data tell us about our original question? Are the results as you expected? Take a moment to think about what I have asked. (Pause) I am looking for someone sitting beautifully with their hand in the air. Thank you, Suzy! What do you think?
Suzy:	The graph shows that the most popular hobby in our class is cycling.
Mrs Simmons:	Well done Suzy! Now who can tell me how she knew that? John, your hand is up and you are sitting well in your seat – what do you think?

One could argue that Mr Jones has been consistent in his expectation that children will not shout out in his class. How he chooses to deal with this is another matter entirely. His rather negative approach seeks to dismiss Will's answer rather than enable Will to regulate his behaviour and, as a consequence, contribute effectively to the discussion. In addition to this, Will is undermined as Mr Jones asks another pupil for the answer, creating a negative response and attitude in Will. Finally, removing Will's hard-earned merit points further aggravates the situation and alienates the relationship between the child and the teacher.

STOP

Looking for and responding to negative behaviours only goes to consolidate the behaviour we do not want. If Mr Jones had allowed Will the opportunity to regulate his behaviour, Will would have learned that responding positively to Mr Jones's expectations would have resulted in a more positive outcome. Any rewards given to children earlier in the day should not be later removed in response to a separate incident.

Mrs Simmons, on the other hand, makes her expectations explicit before asking for the children's responses. Her use of positive language instils in them the behaviour she expects. Her positive approach clearly reaps positive rewards.

Your response to question 2 in the audit you carried out may be directly influenced by your own upbringing. The way in which your behaviour was managed by your parents and/or carers has a real bearing and influence on how you manage the behaviour of children you work with. For instance, there might be particular elements of your childhood that are reflected in your teaching – this could be exemplified in your practice. Were you always expected to say 'please' and 'thank you' as a child? Do you have the same expectations of the children you teach?

The purpose of question 3 – can you think of five words you associate with behaviour management? – is designed to raise your awareness of the wealth of language and terminology associated with behaviour management. Whilst this section cannot define every phrase or term, the following, presented by Hayes (2006: 86), is a guide to the 'core three':

- Behaviour is what the child does.
- Discipline consists of the structures the adult imposes to assist the child's behaviour.
- Control is what the child is learning to exercise to bring about satisfactory behaviour.

ACTIVITY

How many of the following terms do you know, use and understand?

Ethos	Behaviour regulation	Perception	Climate
Contract	Reprimands	Punishment	Incentives
Constructive criticism	Conflict	Privileges	Motivation
Intervention	Self-discipline	Boundaries	Consistency

> Select two or three of those of which you have limited understanding and discuss these with colleagues or peers.

In question 4 you considered the behaviours you have recently encountered in your setting? How many of these behaviours were positive in nature? If we are not careful, we can become cynical about behaviour and focus more on the behaviours that we do not want rather than those we do. Whilst it is easy to identify those behaviours deemed inappropriate, let us take the positive perspective and acknowledge those behaviours we favour in children.

CONSIDERATIONS

Take a look at the following behaviours. Which ones have you responded to recently?

- Curiosity
- Honesty
- Turn-taking
- Motivation
- Warmth
- Listening
- Sharing
- Empathy
- Confidence
- Independence
- Biting
- Arrogance
- Stealing
- Pinching
- Rudeness
- Shouting out
- Name-calling
- Moodiness

How did you do? Have you responded to more positive or negative behaviours? What does this say about your practice? Responding to the positive behaviours instils a calm, caring ethos which encourages pupils to look for intrinsic rewards because they feel positive about themselves. In Chapter 3 we explore these behaviours more thoroughly.

QUESTIONS

6. How many children are there in your class?
7. How many boys? How many girls?

> 8. How many children present inappropriate behaviours?
> 9. When do these behaviours manifest themselves?
> 10. Are there external influences that affect the children's behaviour?

The number of children we teach directly impacts on how well we manage the children's behaviour. The more children we have in our class, the less time we have to get to know the children and their individual personalities, so there is less opportunity for them to connect with their class teacher. Building these relationships through quality interaction on a one-to-one, group and whole-class basis allows teachers and children to work together effectively. Chapter 4 considers ways in which we might develop positive relationships with the children we teach.

The dynamics of the class will be directly influenced by the weighting of gender. Having more boys is likely to present a more boisterous, kinaesthetic and competitive driven environment. Conversely, a larger proportion of girls results in chatter, unnecessary disagreements but at the same time greater empathy. Of course these are generalizations and not all these traits should be necessarily regarded in a negative light.

It is easy to categorize a number of children as being badly behaved. Chances are, if we really analyse our pupils we will find there are only one or two children who really pose us challenges. During the average day there are low-level disruptions which all class teachers face because children will be children. Our own emotional well-being will impact on our perception of the children we teach. Again, this will be further explored in Chapter 4.

Children are more likely to lapse in concentration at the end of the day, often losing motivation, and we can easily misjudge this; therefore matching activities to every need, including that of tiredness, is essential for good behaviour. This is not to say that children's behaviour in the morning will not be inappropriate. A number of factors can affect this, such as how much sleep the child has had, whether they have had breakfast or not, whether the atmosphere at home is one that creates a positive and calming influence on the child or whether they live in a disharmonious environment. Some children naturally feel anxious about school, others lack motivation and some children simply dislike leaving home to go to school early in the morning. Out-of-school clubs and private day care fulfil a specific need for working parents/carers; however, these can often have a negative effect, as the children who attend them may be unhappy, unstimulated or simply exhausted by the length of day.

Many children display poor behaviour as a result of experiences and consequences that occur during playtimes throughout the day. You may need to allow for time after each break to give the children the opportunity to refocus and meet expectations linked to behaviour for the classroom. Chapter 6 explores the nature of working with midday staff.

Particular subject areas which form part of the curriculum require different methods of behaviour management. The effectiveness of this management is dependent upon the type of activities being undertaken, the structure of the session, the type of resources being used to support the learning and the way in which the children are grouped. Learning which involves active participation, interaction and collaboration will engage and motivate pupils but may also lead to excitement and noise, creating a potentially stressful environment for the teacher. Careful management of these activities, where expectations are made explicit and misbehaviour is dealt with consistently, is likely to provide a more purposeful and harmonious working environment. Lessons involving physical activity, such as PE, require a distinct series of behaviour management strategies to ensure the children are safe in the environment and learning skills effectively. Establishing clear expectations even before the children have left the classroom is the starting point of success. Chapter 7 examines this a little further, in relation to dance.

REFLECT

Consider a lesson you have taught recently in which the children's behaviour was a cause for concern. Take a few moments to reflect on your responses to the following questions:

- How clear were your expectations of the children's behaviour?
- Was the lesson appropriately planned, structured and delivered?
- Were the activities matched effectively to the learning needs of the children?
- Were you fully prepared before the actual lesson?
- Did the children understand what they had to do, both in terms of activity and behaviour?
- How did you react to inappropriate behaviour?
- How might you change this for the future?
- Were there other factors which impacted on this lesson?

There are many external factors which can influence the behaviour of children in our classrooms. Children's diets, TV habits, medication and role models are all considerations which we often do not realize have an adverse effect on children's behaviour. Being aware of these and considering ways to manage these factors is important if we are to encourage children to be well behaved. Of course, whatever you do in your class can only be truly effective if there is a common message throughout the school.

School philosophy and context

Every school has a mission statement and this directly influences the way in which behaviour is managed through the school.

CONSIDERATIONS

- School philosophies are often borne out of inspiration and theories that have impacted on the head teacher and the staff.
- School mission statements are often the vision of the head teacher.
- In some schools the mission statement is formulated through a consultation process involving children, parents/carers, school staff and governors.

QUESTIONS

- How is the school mission statement reflected in the behaviour management policy of your school?
- Are there ways in which you can have an impact on ensuring that all children in your care are aware of this statement?
- Where is the mission statement displayed?
- How often do you refer to it?

School philosophies are led by the behaviour management policy, namely by the content, the way it is formulated and the way the policy is put into practice. This notion will be discussed in more detail in Chapter 5.

STOP

Every class teacher will manage the behaviour of the children they teach in a different way. What is important is that there is a shared and agreed understanding which provides a common message for all children as they progress through school. This message should be shared with everyone from midday supervisors to cleaners and senior management.

School philosophies should not be allowed to become stagnant; they are designed to reflect the attitudes, thinking and values of all stakeholders and should be reviewed, evaluated and revised regularly. They should reflect the society of today, embrace change and respond to current recommendations from national bodies. Have you noticed that when you visit different schools they have a different 'feel'? We refer to this as the personality of the school, and every school has a different personality. What is the personality of your school?

ACTIVITY

Take a moment to look at the questions in the diagram below:

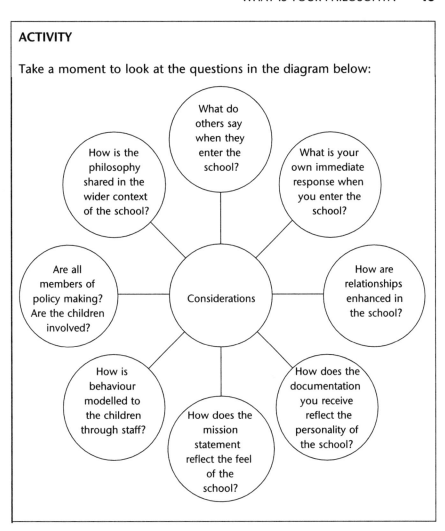

What have you found out about the personality of your school? What aspects of attitude and beliefs may need to be adapted in order to make you and others feel part of the team.

We have looked at the ways in which documentation, pupils, schools and external factors have an impact on pupil behaviour. Now let us think about you.

Where are you and why?

The ways in which you manage behaviour are directly influenced by your past observations and experiences in the classroom. These may be positive or not so positive, as highlighted in the following case studies:

CASE STUDIES

A child came in from playtime crying because her friends did not play the game she wanted to play. The teacher asked all of the children involved about what had happened and listened carefully to their responses. He then asked the children how the situation could have turned out better, to stop Lucy feeling upset, and allowed each child to offer a suggestion. These suggestions were then practised in a role-play situation and the solution was found as a result of communicating with the whole group.

A teacher came into class late having been on the telephone for most of her dinner break. A child whispered something to his friend and suddenly the teacher began shouting at the child, making him stand up whilst she chastised him in front of the rest of the class. The child began to cry and in response to this the teacher told him to 'stop being a cry baby'. The class were set some low-level tasks as it was Friday afternoon. The crying child refused to engage with any activities and cried for the rest of the day.

REFLECT

- How did the teachers' reactions enable or hinder the effective management of the situations described?
- Consider the different ways in which the children involved were affected positively or negatively by the management strategies used by the teachers.
- How could the teachers have responded differently to both situations?
- Is it OK to sometimes raise your voice? Discuss your thinking with a colleague or one of your peers. Make a list of occasions when you would consider it to be 'acceptable' to be stern with a child and offer some suggestions for making this a positive learning experience.

Key points to note are as follows:

- Talking through issues is a very effective way to manage behavioural issues – practitioner mediation is a valued approach to adopt as good practice.
- Allowing every child to have their say is essential.
- Listening to every child is key.
- Create opportunities for children to learn how to put the good practice into operation.
- Avoid shouting wherever possible, but if you do have to shout use a lower, calm voice as quickly as you can to make children aware of how disappointed you are with their behaviour, pointing out the consequences of their actions.

Many educationalists, including Cole *et al.* (2000) and Daniels and Williams (2000), attribute a series of teacher characteristics which they claim to be common to successful practice. Identifying what these characteristics are is a good way to initiate your own thinking about behaviour management and how to develop it for the future.

ACTIVITY

Make a list of the characteristics of effective teachers when they are managing children's behaviour. Consider the following to support you:

- characteristics of your teachers when you were at school;
- characteristics of teachers with whom you have observed or worked;
- characteristics of yourself which may impact on how you deal with behaviour.

Recognizing what these characteristics are is actually very different from how they are used in the classroom – knowing them is not enough. All of these characteristics have their own time and place; some will be more useful than others so the trick is identifying which characteristic is appropriate at a given time with the particular group of children you are teaching. Added to this is the complexity of who you are in a personal and professional sense; you may not feel comfortable adopting certain characteristics but you may well be able to adapt, change and develop some of these to suit who you are as a teacher. By doing this you push yourself out of your comfort zone without preventing yourself from engaging with the pupils.

CASE STUDY

Miss Jack, a third-year student, is on her final teaching placement. Her behaviour management strategies are generally very successful and she rarely struggles to get the children back on task. On one particular day, however, the children are more talkative and difficult to settle than usual. The behaviour management strategies that Miss Jack has previously used are not working and, as a result, she starts to raise her voice. Her mentor comments at break: 'Are you OK today? You don't normally raise your voice.' But in the following lesson the mentor further comments on the children's behaviour and suggests Miss Jack adopt her strategy of singing the instructions. Miss Jack is uncomfortable with this strategy as she feels it may make her look silly but observes her mentor using it with the children and decides to try it out.

'Everybody put your pencils down!' Miss Jack sings and the children do exactly as she has asked. Later that week, when she reflects on her development, Miss Jack notes that although she did not feel comfortable with the strategy at first, having used it a number of times she now feels more able to embrace this approach.

NOTE

Be prepared to step out of your comfort zone – sometimes you have to do this to develop your skills and capabilities.

We asked you to compile a list of effective characteristics, and we too have done this. Compare you list with ours, which overlaps some of the thinking identified by OFSTED (1999a), Cole *et al.* (1998) and Rogers (1997):

( ) Sense of humour   ( ) Understands individual needs
( ) Consistency   ( ) Adaptable
( ) Enthusiasm   ( ) Clear rules
( ) Positive attitude   ( ) Empathetic
( ) Organized   ( ) Positive reinforcement
( ) Firm but fair   ( ) Calm and relaxed
( ) Good listener   ( ) Eclectic responses
( ) Interested in pupils and their   ( ) Promotes resilience
    learning   ( ) Passionate about their subject
( ) Interactive teaching strategies   ( ) High expectations of pupils
( ) Well planned and prepared   ( ) Good role model
( ) Patient

We would like you now to rank-order these characteristics, 1 being the most effective and 22 being the least. Your top five will have a direct impact on the way in which you view and manage pupils' behaviour. Reflect on the analysis of our top five below and compare them with your own.

1. Consistency – being consistent ensures that everybody has the same message. Inconsistency will result in poor behaviour, confusion and unease in the classroom.
2. High expectations – pupils will rise to meet your expectations as long as they are realistic. Low expectations promote poor behaviour by not aspiring to be the best that one can be.
3. Well planned and prepared – being well prepared can pre-empt and prevent poor behaviour. If lessons are pacy, well resourced, structured and interactive pupils do not have the opportunity to misbehave.
4. Interested in pupils and their learning – this point works on two levels, the child as a person and the child as a learner. By knowing who your children are, their interests, friends and family, you can plan activities and lessons to engage pupils. This leads on to the child as a learner: by knowing the child you plan not only to meet their personal interests but also their learning needs through learning and teaching styles.
5. Sense of humour – every teacher needs a sense of humour. Your sense of humour

will sometimes be your saving grace; this does not mean that you have to be a stand-up comedian. Your humour will need to suit the age you are working with; for example, Key Stage 2 pupils respond more readily to puns and witticisms, whereas children in the early years enjoy nonsense rhymes and silly words – 'squigglehop'. Leave the sarcasm at home as it really does not have a place in the primary school classroom.

Analysis of this top five has hopefully provided you with a further opportunity to appreciate the complexities of the characteristics of the effective teachers you have come across during your experience in school. Of course, our top five is borne out of our own personal experience in a variety of educational settings. These may change as our experience and knowledge develops. Our top five may be different from your top five, given the context within which you find yourself, but what is important is that you can identify the 'why' of a strategy or characteristic as opposed to simply the 'what'. We will explore this notion further in Chapter 3.

KEY POINTS

- Every child matters – and so do the teachers. Embrace change and embrace the agenda so it has a direct impact on children's lives and behaviour.
- Philosophies operate on a national, regional, school and classroom level. Ensure parity within these by drawing together good practice and involving all members of the school community.
- Auditing practice: discussion, debate, reflection and analysis are key to establishing the climate and moving practice forward in a positive way.
- Teacher qualities: knowing what a good teacher should be is not enough; deeper analysis through the 'how' and the 'why' will help you to embed these characteristics in your own practice.

2 Putting the practice into theory: child development

This chapter examines the way in which children develop a moral understanding in relation to theoretical perspectives. We will specifically explore:

- theories of moral development;
- internalization and moral understanding;
- how children learn self-control;
- practical ways of putting the theory into practice.

Moral understanding – what does it mean?

Before getting to know how a child becomes a moral being, it might be useful to define what we mean by 'moral'. Reschke (2005) defines it as knowing what should be done and then doing it; 'should' is what is defined by societies, cultures, families and individuals.

Schaffer (1996) suggests that a sense of morality is acquired through distinguishing right from wrong; that one has developed a sense of how to behave in accordance with social order. It is the development of 'inner conviction' (Schaffer 1996: 290) as opposed to fear of punishment that enables one to conduct oneself appropriately. According to Schaffer (1996) internalization of social principles and adult behaviour enables children to develop conscience.

Being moral relies on two tenets – moral reasoning and moral behaviour. Moral reasoning determines what is right or wrong, whereas moral behaviour is about making the right choices, choosing not to do wrong. In order to be a moral person there are many developmental abilities involved. Healthy emotional development is essential; this is further examined in Chapter 4.

QUESTION

What aspects of emotional development do you feel are fundamental in becoming able to reason and behave morally?

Here are some suggested emotional responses that are part of moral development:

- feeling guilty;
- feeling and being motivated by empathy;
- fearing or being aware of negative consequences.

Healthy cognitive development is also essential as this ensures that children can understand the perspectives of others, can link causes and effects and can reason out a moral solution when two moral values are conflicting. Finally, we must consider social development as an integral aspect of morality, since our lives are not lived in isolation from others, and the people with whom we interact shape our moral development and understanding.

Healthy moral development begins at the point of infancy, when we make attachments with our primary caregivers. Children who lack these attachments often display signs of low emotional intelligence, a lack of empathy and an inability to decipher right from wrong – or that they choose to do wrong.

So when we speak of moral development, to what are we referring?

> REFLECT
>
> - How did you learn right from wrong?
> - What was discipline like in your home?
> - How was discipline instilled in school?
> - How has this changed? What are your thoughts on this?
> - What do you think about the way in which children are encouraged to behave in school? At home? In the community?
> - How do the children you work with demonstrate development of their conscience?

Studies of very young children and their mothers have shown that normally developing infants are able to respond to their mother's mood and match it. When a mother smiles and coos at her infant, the child responds by kicking their legs and staring intently. If the mother expresses anger or unhappiness, the child will initially stare intently, smile and act happy. When the mother does not change her mood, the child turns away in distress (Reschke 2005).

Infants very quickly develop an understanding of mood through facial expression and vocalization. By the age of 4 months, infants can usually distinguish between happy, sad and angry facial expressions. By 8 months, their emotional intelligence has become quite sophisticated. Babies can distinguish between facial expressions and voices that match in terms of their emotional content. Mixed messages can confuse babies and by the age of 1 year they are able to recognize a mismatch in the facial expression and vocalization.

Emotional knowledge enables children to develop an understanding of morality at a quicker rate. Emotional knowledge relates to when we point out the behaviour children demonstrate, and positively label that behaviour at the point it is happening; this is particularly associated with toddlers and preschool children. So when a child is sharing, a parent who says 'Well done Freya, you are so kind to share your pencils' is aiding that child in their emotional knowledge. Children are also more likely to repeat behaviours which are linked to positive experiences.

Moral internalization and the development of the conscience

There comes a point in our development when we recognize what is socially and culturally acceptable or appropriate. However, how does this moral internalization happen? At what point do we develop a conscience?

We discussed earlier how guilt is an important aspect of moral development. Children respond with self-conscious emotions that are connected with the way we feel about ourselves and are an important component in the internalization of moral growth. Guilt, shame and pride are the three most common self-conscious emotions displayed by children.

- *Pride* is what we feel when others view our actions as right and good and praiseworthy.
- *Shame* is what we feel when someone else, especially someone important to us, expresses disapproval of our behaviour.
- *Guilt* is what we feel when we do something wrong and feel personally responsible for the outcome.

(Reschke 2005: 3)

Children tend to express these emotions as they grow up from about the age of 2. These emotions require children to have a sense of self and require adult input about when they are appropriate. These are learned responses and therefore entail a certain level of brain development, hence the age appropriate ability to recognize and respond to the adult input.

NOTE

As infants are exploring and discovering their world, we rarely regard their behaviour as bad behaviour. We tend to see it as learning about the world in which they live and as their behaviour is not an intentional disregard for rules or acceptable codes of conduct we do not view it in the same way. Because of this, from a young age, children learn to respond to praise and, consequently, pride is the first of the three self-conscious emotions demonstrated by children.

Shame develops as children begin to understand intent. With intent comes the understanding that the choice made is not always the right choice in terms of what is right and wrong. Parents frown and chastise, their tone is harsher and children cry or cover their faces in response to the punishment.

Guilt is demonstrated around the age of 3. Children deem some of their behaviour as wrong, even if it was unintentional. If they accidentally break a cup or spill a drink, young children will feel guilt and think they have done wrong. This links to the fact that children at this age are still incapable of associating guilt and intention.

Piaget's theory of moral development

Piaget (1932) believed that all development transpires from action; that children build their knowledge of the world through interactions with the environment in which they find themselves. It was Piaget's belief that moral understanding was a developmental process, and, with this in mind, he developed a stage theory consisting of three levels of progression – *premoral, moral realism* and *moral subjectivism*. During the premoral stage – up to 4 years of age – children have no understanding of rules or of the basis of right and wrong (Schaffer 1996). During the moral realism stage – from the age of 4 to 9–10 years of age – actions are judged by material outcome. Rules become sacred and cannot be changed and ethical judgements are based on consequences rather than interventions (Short 1999). Children in this phase of development also believe in 'immanent justice' – that punishment should immediately follow acts of wrongdoing. From the age of 9–10, children move into the moral subjectivism phase; they begin to judge actions in relation to the intention and there is an understanding that rules can be changed if there is mutual agreement. When children reach this stage of moral development they have internalized the social rules and boundaries and can operate in the adult world with an understanding of how to behave according to their social setting.

NOTE

According to Piaget (1932), progression from a stage where there is incomprehension of rules and moral judgements to a stage of being capable of understanding intent, justice and authority depends on two factors: the child's cognitive abilities and their social experiences.

Kohlberg's theory of moral development

Kohlberg's theory was based on the stage theory of Piaget. As Piaget's work was limited in terms of the transition from moral realism to moral subjectivism and as children's moral understanding seemed to progress no further after mid-childhood, he modified and elaborated on Piaget's work. His theory also consisted of three levels, but he identified six stages of moral development, two stages within each of the three levels.

At the first level, the *preconventional* level, stage one (punishment and obedience orientation), the focus is on obedience to those in authority, wrongdoing being punishable, and, as in Piaget's theory, there is no conception of rules. By stage two (individualism and instrumental orientation) the child is following rules only when it is in their immediate interest.

Individuals at level two, the *conventional morality* level, have a basic understanding of norms and conventions and can reason that these are necessary to uphold society. By stage three of this level children become aware of shared feelings; being good relates to trust, loyalty and respect. The perspective tends to be kept within the family or the community as an understanding of the wider social field has not yet developed. This view of the larger social system develops at stage four, and being a 'good' member of society is important. Piaget's moral subjectivism relates to this stage where children have a more sophisticated view and understanding of rules and socially acceptable behaviour.

The final level in Kohlberg's theory is the *postconventional level*. Individuals operating at this level have a sound understanding of rules and their function, but by the time they reach stage six, moral judgement involves reasoning rooted in ethical fairness. There is an understanding that regard for life and human welfare are to be upheld regardless of other conventions (Nucci 2002).

Both Kohlberg and Piaget were interested in the role of 'intent' in moral development. In order to ascertain the level or stage at which a child was operating, Kohlberg and Piaget used a story paradigm. Piaget used pairs of stories, each with an undesirable outcome but whereby the result was either due to intentional naughtiness or purely accidental (Schaffer 1996). Let us take as an example the stories of John and Henry.

ACTIVITY

Read the two stories and consider the implications.

John walked into a room. He did not know that behind the door there was a tray of teacups. As the door opened, it bumped the tray and accidentally broke fifteen cups.

Henry wanted some jam. His mother said no and put the jam on a high shelf out of his reach. Henry climbed up and knocked a cup from the shelf. The cup broke.

Who is more naughty, John or Henry?

This may seem like an easy answer to us, because we are aware of intention. At some stage in our development we have learned that accidents happen, but we also know that by intentionally making the wrong choice there are consequences to face.

As children move from the premoral stage to the stage of moral realism, they conclude that John was the more naughty of the two because he has done more damage. As children begin to understand intent, they find Henry to be the more naughty as he is aware of the motive behind his behaviour. Piaget's choice of methodology and levels of damage in each story has been criticized by other researchers. Rest (1983) suggests that children are able to make decisions about intention at a much earlier age. Imamoğlu (1975) presented children with similar stories, but in these the damage remained constant – it was only the levels of intention that were varied. The conclusion reached was that children of a much younger age than that proposed by Piaget were able to understand motive and intent (Schaffer 1996). One could also question the ages that Piaget used in his stages of moral development.

Although Piaget stated that cognitive ability and social experience enabled progression through these stages, there is little attention paid to the individual circumstances of children. The way in which they have been directed at home by parents and carers and the social setting in which the child is brought up will inevitably play an important role in their moral competence. Some children will undoubtedly progress through the stages at a greater rate than others, depending on previous guidance, advice and experience.

As is true with all aspects of moral development, there is a gradual movement toward internalization with self-conscious emotions. In the preschool year, children often only feel guilt, shame or pride when there is an adult present. This person is the social referent – someone who gives them cues to how they should feel about a particular behaviour. Once children begin to adopt adult standards for behaviour as their own, they begin to feel self-conscious emotions regardless of the presence of others.

Kohlberg (1969) also used stories containing moral dilemmas in his methodology. One example is the 'Heinz' story that was posed to children.

ACTIVITY

A pharmacist discovered a cure for a special kind of cancer and was selling the drug at ten times the cost it took to make. A man (Heinz) whose wife was dying of the particular cancer in question made a plea bargain with the pharmacist. He asked the pharmacist to sell it at a lower price as he had so little money. The pharmacist refused and insisted on full payment. In a desperate attempt to save his wife's life, the man broke into the shop and stole the drug.

REFLECT

This story is more complex as there are more issues to consider.

- What do you think?
- Who was right?
- Is there a right answer?
- What might children say?

Children operating in the early stages of moral development, the preconventional level, considered the action as wrongdoing, and reasoning on ethical grounds was not apparent. Later, as children had developed an understanding for human welfare and justice, their moral judgements changed and they offered reasoning and more sophisticated arguments for the ethical implications in the story, showing a progression into the higher levels of moral reasoning and understanding.

Like Piaget, Kohlberg's work was criticized for its methodology. The stories were deemed to be highly complex, and with so many ethical issues integrated in them, arguably the key aspect of the moral stories could be lost within the sub-issues. Eisenberg (1986) made the criticism that these stories tended to deal with the wrongdoing, leaving other moral decisions out on a limb, devoid of the discussion that they merited. Although Kohlberg sought to rectify the limited age bracket that Piaget based his work on, his research has been criticized for its bias towards males.

Gilligan (1982) suggested that girls think differently than boys, that their orientation is towards caregiving and nurturing, and that their concern for this side of human nature implies that they approach moral dilemmas from a different viewpoint than that of their male counterparts.

QUESTIONS

Consider pupils in your class.

- Do girls behave differently than boys?
- Do girls demonstrate a more caring side?
- Did the boys and girls respond differently to the stories?

In order to act morally, it could be argued that one has to understand what is deemed to be moral behaviour. It could also be argued that understanding moral behaviour implies that one will act morally. However, is this actually the case? 'One can reason in terms of principles and not live up to those principles' (Kohlberg 1975 quoted in Schaffer 1996: 300).

Read the following scenarios and consider the ways in which the children have developed some moral understanding. Consider both children in your reflection of their moral development.

SCENARIO

During playtime, Martha, aged 4, ran into school shouting her teacher's name. 'Mr Birkett, Mr Birkett, Simon stepped on my sandcastle. He said it was an accident but I know it wasn't – he did it on purpose!'

- How would you deal with this?
- What information do you need?
- How can you ensure similar incidents do not occur?

- What clues are there in the use of the children's language that demonstrate their understanding of moral behaviour?

During a game of chess in the lunchtime club, Chloe was upset because her game with Alice was disturbed when a boisterous child knocked the chess pieces from the board. Chloe was convinced the boy had done it on purpose but Joe remained steadfast – it was an accident and he was sorry.

- How would you ensure you found the underlying cause of the incident?
- How would you pacify Chloe?
- What systems would you put in place to ensure the same thing did not happen again?
- How would you reconcile the children?
- Do both children display signals that point to their understanding of moral conduct?

Kohlberg believed that there was more likely to be consistency between knowledge and behaviour as an individual reaches the higher levels of moral development. This link between knowledge and behaviour has implications for educational practice. Hartshorne and May (1928–30), in their 'Character Education Inquiry' involving children aged 8–16, investigated children's temptation to be dishonest in a variety of situations ranging from stealing to cheating on tests. Their research found that there was little consistency in moral conduct and that an individual's honesty is influenced by many other factors. So how does this link to moral education in the classroom? It would seem that although children have an understanding of moral codes, they do not necessarily live by them.

Socialization plays a vital role in children's moral development and the parenting techniques that a child has experienced will have an impact on the way in which they behave in environments different to home, such as school.

NOTE

Hoffman (1978, 1988) grouped parenting techniques under three headings:
- love-oriented discipline, where parents withhold affection and approval in order to encourage children to conform;
- power-assertive discipline, where parents rely on superior power over the child;
- inductive discipline, which is a non-punitive technique, providing explanation and a cognitive rationale to encourage the child to conform.

These techniques are also recognizable in classrooms:
- Which technique do you adopt?
- Are you aware of others who adopt other techniques?
- Which technique do think is most effective and why?

In a study by Hoffman and Salzstein (1967), it was found that inductive discipline was the most effective in enabling children to internalize moral standards. If this is the case in parenting, could the same be said for teachers? Mayall (1999) suggests that children have to make an important transition when they begin school, from the identity they have at home to the one that they develop in the school setting. James (1993) refers to this identity as the 'schoolchild'. In developing socialization in the classroom, teachers have to pay attention to a number of factors: grouping, organization, and monitoring performance and behaviour. Can inductive discipline have the same effect in school as it does at home? It would seem that through the use of positive behaviour policies, to some extent this could be the case; however, as Mayall (1999) suggests, schools devalue the self-care routines that children have learned at home and children have to relearn the routines to fit into the school systems that are adult-directed.

QUESTIONS

- How does your school ensure that children are able to apply positive behaviour they have learned at home to the school environment?
- Can children make some choices about routines in school, or are they expected to join in at every level?
- Is it always practical to do so?
- What changes could you reasonably make?

Piaget believed that moral education should emphasize co-operative decision-making and problem-solving. He suggested that teachers should provide children with opportunities for personal discovery, rather than teaching norms (Nucci 2002).

Using peer and self intervention

We know that children learn from one another and that sometimes they can be more responsive to their peers than they are to their teachers. Providing opportunities for children to regulate their own behaviour and for others to help them can be a useful way to encourage and build up self-control.

TOP TIPS

- Provide opportunities for dialogue between children to talk about good behaviour.

- Thinking time. Allow time for children to think

- Peer mediation. This has a no-blame approach and finds a win–win outcome to a situation.

- Provide children with the task of spotting good

- Pair a child who sometimes forgets how to behave with someone who always behaves nicely.

- Provide collaborative opportunities for tasks,

about their behaviour and ways to rectify it. If necessary, ask them to talk to a friend.	behaviour and noting it in the behaviour book. At the end of the lesson, names can be read out.	where the outcome is dependent on children having an input.

Self-control

Of course, for internalization to happen effectively, young people need to be able to self-evaluate and consider what is deemed right. There cannot always be an adult present to direct children's behaviour.

We well remember those days as either a trainee teacher or a qualified one when we have seen children act differently. Consider the following scenario:

SCENARIO

Miss Williamson is in her final year of training. During the last three placements, she has been commended for her excellent use of behaviour management strategies to create a positive and purposeful working environment. In the last week, she has been working 'solo' with the Year 5 class with whom she has been placed. In the previous week, her mentor had been in and out of the classroom during Miss Williamson's teaching sessions and the children were aware of the teacher's presence. Today the class teacher is on a course and the children know that Miss Williamson is on her own. As the children enter the classroom, she follows her usual routine of greeting them. They politely say good morning until Mark enters the classroom. 'Good morning, Mark' she says as he comes in, 'Morning Miss Williambum' he replies. Miss Williamson is most surprised as he is usually very well mannered. 'Mark, you wouldn't say that if Mrs Bradley were here, now would you?' He takes a moment to think and says 'No, because she would give me a yellow card.'

- What should Miss Williamson do?
- Would you also give Mark a yellow card?
- Would you talk to him about his behaviour and warn him that if he is rude again he will receive a yellow card?
- Would you shout at him?
- Would you ask if anything had happened before he came into school?

She decides to give him a yellow card and quickly settles the class in order to take the register. During registration, he continues in the same vein, mimicking her and laughing with his friends. She perseveres and

> once the register is taken she sets the children to work. She asks Mark to come and talk to her. He tells her that on the playground some of the boys had dared him to be rude as Mrs Bradley was away and Miss Williamson would not be as cross.
>
> - What do you do now?
> - Do you find out who the other culprits are?
> - Do you give the boys a yellow card too?
> - Do you give Mark a red card?
>
> Miss Williamson does all of these things and then speaks to the whole class about her expectations and how they should behave well, whether or not their teacher is present. She asks Mark and the other boys to think about their behaviour and how they might put the situation right. The boys apologize and say they will work hard for the rest of the day with no more nonsense. At playtime, they offer to pick up all the coats.

By maintaining a consistent approach in her own expectations as well as those of Mrs Bradley, Miss Williamson and the children had a successful day in school. Of course, there are days when the behaviour of children can get us down and we do not always have such flourishing outcomes. Be aware of what happens on these days and reflect on the different situations occurring. You can then put systems in place ready for the next day or, indeed, that afternoon. Do not be defeated and remember that it is not always the fault of the children. Chapter 4 explores our emotional intelligence in greater detail and provides some coping strategies.

Primary children evaluate themselves in a range of contexts. They acquire a sense of whether they are accepted by peers, family and teachers. Some develop an internal locus of control, a feeling that one has the power to regulate one's own life. Others develop an external locus of control, a belief that one is mainly powerless and unable to make a difference. Feelings of moral self-worth – that is, of being a good or bad person – are formed. Hence, children hold many distinct types of self-esteem during the primary years.

We should show that we unconditionally care for the children in our classrooms. By being responsive, showing interest, and being warm, we can enhance feelings of acceptance. We should give over to children as much control of the classroom as is possible. Children should be encouraged to solve social or learning problems independently. A group decision-making process can be implemented in which all children in the class participate in selecting projects or topics to study. A group meeting could be held several times a week to air worries or to raise and solve problems in the classroom. These experiences lead to an internal locus of control in that they help children learn that they have power over their own lives.

Moral behaviour is about making choices. Self-control is about reasoning oneself through a moral dilemma. With self-control comes the ability to resist temptation. When there are external factors involved, such as a punishment or a negative consequence, children find it easier to resist the temptation. What we are aiming for in school is that children will learn to respond to intrinsic motivation rather than extrinsic incentives. This applies as much to reward as it does to punishment.

Although we advocate the use of stickers and stars as rewards for good behaviour, we also advocate the use of non-material rewards that relate to the desired behaviour. Children are very aware of their feelings of guilt and shame – the self-conscious emotions of which we spoke earlier. They know how these feelings make them feel inside. It is as important to help children to understand what we feel like inside when they are being good, so they feel pride – another self-conscious emotion.

The mental foundations for self-control (see Reschke 2005: 4) are:

- the ability to think of oneself as an independent person, able to control one's own behaviour;
- the memory capacity to recall earlier instructions or commands, especially in the presence of temptation;
- the mental ability to ignore some stimuli in the environment (the tempting thing) while focusing on other, more positive stimuli;
- the ability of strategies for resisting temptation, such as distraction, repeating the instructions out loud, or reciting to oneself the rewards of compliance and consequences of non-compliance.

Understanding the consequences of behaviour and actions are a large part of learning self-control. This applies to both how an action may have an adverse affect on oneself and also how an action may have an adverse affect on another individual.

REFLECT

Take three routines you have adopted in your classroom.

- Think about how the rule patterns associated with these routines were made. If you did these with the children, consider how well the routines work.
- What do the children do in order to maintain these routines effectively?
- How might they be revised to be more effective?

If you created the routines without the input of your class, think about how well they work. Do the children do as they have been asked simply because they know it is what you expect, or do they carry them out because they want to? How might you change your practice to involve your pupils in routines and patterns in the classroom?

Other points of view

Moral development requires the ability to see things from the perspective of another person. This is not an easy task for us as adults, but especially for children. Fisher (1995) believes that this leap of imagination is fundamental in moral development and to an understanding of others; he calls it 'interpersonal intelligence'. By considering both sides of a conflict and encouraging children to consider their own stance, we can help them to understand how other people feel in the same situation. Therefore they resolve the conflict more successfully. The following tasks encourage seeing things from another's point of view.

ACTIVITY

List what you think are the views of different people in these examples from Fisher (1995: 83):

- You lend a friend some money to buy a lottery ticket. Your friend wins a prize. Who does the prize belong to? What might be the different points of view of you and your friend?
- A father and mother forbid their son and daughter to stay up past 10 o'clock to watch a television programme. What are the points of view of the children and the parents?
- A burglar breaks into your house and steals everything of value. Your parents phone the police. What are the views of your parents, the police and the burglar?

A simple but effective way of helping children to understand the consequences of their actions is to provide them with a range of different outcomes for their behaviour. Understanding what might happen as a result of making one choice rather than another may enable them to consider the best solution to their problem. Consider the following:

SCENARIO

Inderjit is having her 8th birthday party. She wants to invite her closest friends, but she knows that Tom and Rupinder do not really get along. She would like them both to be there but does not want to create tension or problems at the party for any of the other children, herself, Tom or Rupinder. She tells her teacher. Miss Charles suggests she weighs up all the options in the following way, using a Carroll diagram:

	Invite Rupinder	**Don't invite Rupinder**
Invite Tom	They might argue and spoil the party.	Then Rupinder will be upset but everybody will get along.
Don't invite Tom	Tom might be upset but there would be no arguments.	I won't enjoy the party because neither friend will be there.

Inderjit decides to invite Tom and to have a special day with Rupinder before the party. Rupinder and Inderjit have a day out roller-skating and a special lunch.

By seeing all the options, Inderjit is able to make a decision about how her choice will affect everybody. Eventually, as she adopts adult values and understanding, Inderjit will learn to make these decisions internally. What is most important here is that she can make a decision that will create a happy outcome for her and her friends whilst considering the feelings of all the children involved.

- Consider how you might use this strategy with your class.
- What are the benefits of such a strategy? The pitfalls?
- How might the strategy be transposed into different situations?

By being provided with practical solutions to moral dilemmas, children quickly learn to self-regulate behaviour, to recognize and understand the way others feel and to apply these strategies to other situations with which they may be faced. By giving people choices we empower them. That sense of empowerment is important. McCune *et al.* (1999) define 'locus of control' as the degree to which learners feel that events they experience are under their control (internal control), rather than under the control of other people or forces outside of themselves (external control). We can relate this to the successes that young people feel they have control of in school in terms of their subject development or, indeed, of their experiences in their social contexts.

Of course, not all children respond in the ways we would hope and sometimes we have to take a firm stance. How you approach it in your own classroom will be influenced by a number of things. Here are some examples:

- The style of discipline that parents adopt at home will have an impact on the way particular children respond to specific styles of behaviour management.
- A child's conscience takes time to develop and will depend on the different situations they have experienced. Encourage children to listen to their inner self and to respond to it in a safe environment.
- We can use stories to enable moral development. Stories that have moral

dilemmas included or where difficult decisions have to be made are particularly good for helping children understand causes and effects.

- Children are not passive in rule learning. Involve them in making rules and systems that will work for everybody. They are less likely to break rules they have created themselves.
- Use an inductive style of discipline in the classroom, which involves appealing to understanding rather than emotions and fears.

Special educational needs

Some children may suffer serious emotional disturbance (SED), autism, or attention deficit hyperactivity disorder (ADHD) in the primary years, conditions that often lead to peer rejection. A variety of causes and remediation strategies have been proposed for these disorders. New techniques for promoting trust and attachment, facilitating friendships, encouraging verbal and non-verbal communication, and helping children interpret social situations are effective ways in enabling children to 'fit in' in the social environments and to be better accepted by their peers.

We need to be familiar with and able to identify the characteristics of children with SED, autism, and ADHD. Negative affect, harsh and often aggressive reactions to others, antisocial or withdrawn behaviour, and conduct problems in school are common among children with SED. Children who avoid contact, even eye contact, with others, speak very little, and perform repetitive, ritualistic behaviours may have autism. Those who are highly active, impulsive, and inattentive in ways that interfere with learning and social interactions may have ADHD. It is recommended that you look for training in these areas in order to further your competence in dealing with particular behaviours.

> NOTE
>
> - We must help all children in a class understand invisible learning difficulties, such as SED, autism, or ADHD.
> - Although these are difficult conditions to explain to young children, an open dialogue about them will increase empathy and caring.
> - When teachers are open about learning difficulties, children will be as well.
> - They will ask questions and more readily enter into relationships with those who have these special needs.

Based on Piaget's theory, Power *et al.* (1989) suggested that moral education in schools required more than individual reflection. He and his colleagues developed the 'just community' schools approach to moral education (Power *et al.* 1989, in Nucci 2002), whereby the pupils were given the opportunity to participate in a democratic community. It was believed that if the responsibility were placed on the pupils, they would take prosocial behaviour more seriously. This approach can be seen in schools today where children form part of the school council and all children have a 'voice' in the decisions that are made in the school. The curriculum also provides opportunity for moral discussion with the introduction of citizenship education, which involves discussion of moral, political and community issues. Children are actively involved in their understanding of change through action, whether it be through their own change or that of others.

Good practice in citizenship education might include:

> opportunities for children to help define rules in their own classroom or to represent each other in the context of a school council; developing a school environmental policy with children and allowing them to help take care of the school buildings and grounds; inviting parents in to talk about their roles in the wider community, as well as visits from members of the local council, or local and national voluntary bodies, to give children an understanding of their work.
>
> (Hinds n.d.)

Discussion is likely to form a major part of citizenship education, perhaps incorporated into the circle time sessions that are now such a feature of many primary schools. Don Rowe, director of curriculum resources at the Citizenship Foundation, says that the quality of teacher questioning in these sessions is vitally important, so that questions are framed in such a way as to deepen children's thinking.

He believes we could be more effective in our questioning if we had a better understanding of what he calls 'moral stage theory'. This relates to the developmental models we have already discussed, in which young children are in the typically egocentric and punishment-oriented phase of morality. For instance, if you ask a young child why it is wrong to steal, they will tend to say, 'because you'll get put in prison'. With guidance later this matures into a more abstract and empathetic understanding, whereby moral rules are more fully internalized. Helping a child on towards this more mature understanding can do a great deal to alleviate self-centred or aggressive behaviour towards others.

Rowe believes that once teachers have an understanding of this, it gives them a framework of questions to pose. For example, empathy-related questions, such as 'how do you think that person would feel?', can help to move children on.

There is little centralized direction from government in exactly how schools go about incorporating citizenship into their timetables. Some give the subject its own weekly slot, but many aspects of the work will overlap with topics raised in the literacy hour, or in geography, history, and religious education. Large areas of citizenship, too, naturally relate to the life and ethos of the whole school, taking shape, for instance, in assemblies or school council meetings. Of course, for primary education, citizenship is yet to be made a statutory subject, yet many schools realize the importance of this area of learning and so teach the principles through the Every Child Matters agenda.

It is important to believe that if every child can have their voice heard, understood and responded to, they will become active participants in their communities. School Councils UK has welcomed the Every Child Matters priorities, and has seen at first hand how the work of school councils within the categories of ECM improves children's lives:

Being healthy

Confidence and communication skills can be developed from being involved with class and School Councils. Pupils can develop emotional resilience. They can also help make their peers healthier by [for example] improving food in the dining room and promoting sports activities and competitions.

Staying safe

Effective School Councils produce peer leadership, openness and awareness. These qualities help to make schools safer and happier places. The most effective anti-bullying schemes are led by pupils.

Enjoying and achieving

By taking the opportunity to become involved in the school community, essential life skills such as listening, diplomacy, compromise and communication are developed.

Effective participation structures in schools help raise attainment by improving the learning environment.

Making a positive contribution

Through School Councils, [pupils'] belief in their ability to make a difference develops. Life skills learned through active participation [enable] pupils to contribute to their local community and wider society.

Achieving economic well being

Many School Councils are given a grant to manage. The responsibility of running a budget helps pupils develop economic and financial awareness.

(Gateshead Healthy Schools n.d.)

Moral development is complex and difficult to measure. What is evident is that children cannot be categorized in stages as all children have different experiences, cultural backgrounds and levels of maturation. In school, children may behave in ways that are deemed to be morally wrong or they may be considered to be socially inept, and the transition between home life and school life could be a factor in moral development. It could be said that children who are actively involved in their moral education learn to internalize and understand social rules at an earlier age and can therefore regulate their behaviour in an appropriate manner for the social setting in which they find themselves.

KEY POINTS

- Children develop moral understanding better when they are involved in the process. Use an inductive style of behaviour management to aid this.
- Use stories as a strategy for developing moral understanding.
- Provide opportunities for children to talk to one another and to collaborate in activities.
- Create a bank of moral dilemmas to use in the classroom so that the children have the opportunity to learn about consequences of actions – cause and effect.
- Be consistent in the messages you give so that children are not confused about what you expect of them.
- Provide a forum for airing views, worries and issues that feed into whole-school systems such as school councils.

3 Behaviour phases through the ages

This chapter centres its attention specifically upon identifying behaviours commonly found in primary classrooms, examining strategies, approaches and thinking to manage them effectively. In particular, it will focus on:

- day-to-day behaviours found in children across the age phases in Key Stages 1 and 2;
- behaviours associated with children who have special educational needs (SEN) common to the primary classroom;
- behaviours associated with transitions.

Whilst the value of the previous two chapters cannot be underestimated, it is important for us now to consider the wealth of different behaviours we are likely to encounter in the classroom on a day-to-day basis, and to begin to reflect critically on how they will be effectively managed. This chapter will build on Chapter 2 by highlighting different approaches to behaviour management within a practical context, whilst challenging your personal philosophy (as developed in Chapter 1) by not only reflecting on the value of various practical strategies and techniques, but also considering the implications of how acquiring specific knowledge, skills and understanding will directly impact on your effectiveness in the classroom. Let us begin this chapter by exploring what every teacher wants and needs to know: what behaviours am I going to face in the classroom on a day-to-day basis?

Day-to-day behaviours found in children across the age phases in Key Stages 1 and 2

ACTIVITY

Consider all of the different behaviours you would expect to see, or that you have seen, in both Key Stage 1 and 2 classrooms. Create a list of these behaviours. Where possible or appropriate, challenge one of your peers or colleagues to engage with this activity, comparing your lists.

Whilst most of you will have found the activity above to be relatively easy to complete, it is important for you to reflect critically on those behaviours you have noted. How many of them would you class as being 'desirable' – the behaviours that we *want* to see in children? It is likely that your lists will actually contain more 'undesirable' behaviours – those we want to actively *discourage* in children, as opposed to those that are more positive or 'good' in nature. The purpose of this reflection is designed to highlight two important points:

1. When thinking about effective behaviour management it is important to focus more on those behaviours which we *want* to see in children as opposed to always thinking you are going to encounter behaviours which are negative or troublesome in some way. This positive 'mind-set' will help you to 'look for the good' in children's behaviour and discourage you from always picking up on negative behaviours exhibited or searching for it.
2. An important aspect of effective behaviour management centres on teachers having a clear understanding of which behaviours they consider to be desirable and undesirable in children.

THINK

Why do you think we have deliberately used the terms 'desirable' and 'undesirable' to distinguish between different forms of behaviour? Would it be appropriate to use the following terms: best, bad, naughty, recommended, poor, perfect? If so, why? If not, why not?

Let us address the second key point made above by comparing your lists of desirable/undesirable behaviours with the list we have compiled – how do they compare?

Desirable behaviours	Undesirable behaviours
• Polite	• Angry
• Happy	• Arrogant
• Keen to contribute	• Rude
• Team player	• Impolite
• Honest	• Selfish
• Hard working	• Violent
• Helpful	• Lying
• Friendly	• Disrespectful
• Well mannered	• Stealing
• Loving	• Bullying tendencies
• Obedient	• Name-calling
• Confident	• Spitting
• Motivated	• Restless
• Curious	• Shouting out

- Good levels of concentration
- Risk taker
- Tidy
- Articulate
- Good listener
- Able to share
- Proud
- Independent

- Moody
- Making sexist/racist comments
- Kicking others
- Nose-picking
- Killing living things
- Deliberately hurting the feelings of others
- Talking over others

Attempting to identify and discuss all behaviours seen in primary classrooms is a near-impossible task because each class will have 30 or more children in it who are all individuals, have individual needs and have individual ways in which they behave. However, the principles of managing behaviours commented on in this chapter are easily transferable to those which are not highlighted, and you are asked to be mindful of this whilst engaging with the rest of this chapter.

It is significant to note that the simple act of identifying behaviours seen in the classroom supports engagement with the first stage of a three-step 'be clear' approach, which is advocated for the effective management of children's behaviour (see Figure 1).

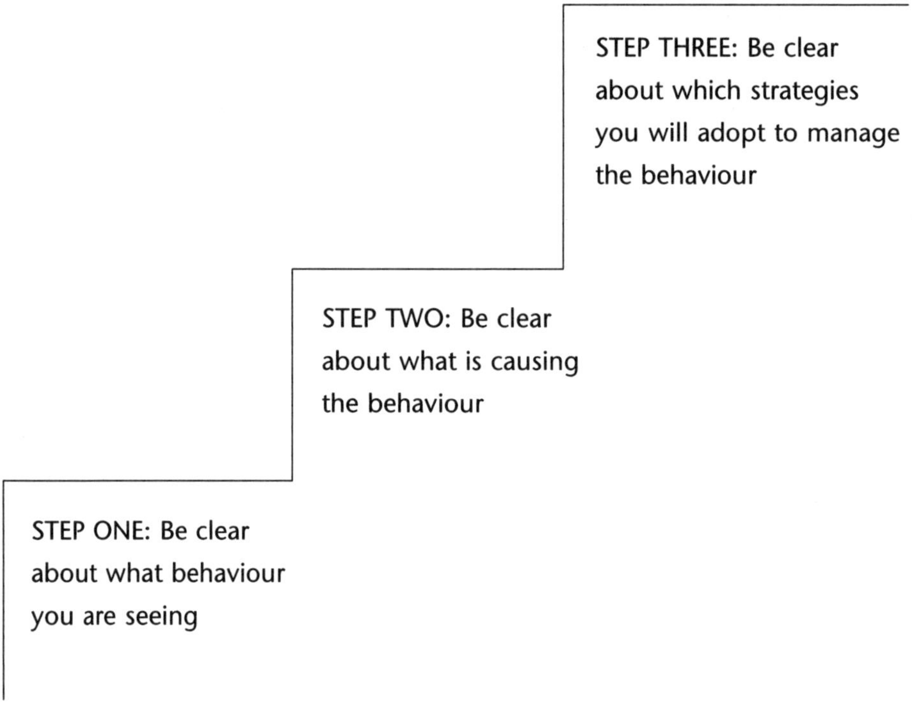

STEP THREE: Be clear about which strategies you will adopt to manage the behaviour

STEP TWO: Be clear about what is causing the behaviour

STEP ONE: Be clear about what behaviour you are seeing

Figure 1 Brownhill's three-step 'be clear' approach

Whilst engagement with step one of the approach is relatively simple, it is essential that you are also able to *define* the behaviours seen so that there is clarity in what exactly is being referred to. Healy (2003: 24) argues that defining behaviours is actually very difficult because we bring 'different experiences, expectations, observations and knowledge to one word'. Nevertheless, a good understanding of the behaviours seen is the first step to its effective management.

> REFLECT
>
> How would you define 'independence'? What about 'aggression'? Can you be 'happy' and 'impolite' at the same time? Discuss your thoughts with a peer or colleague and try to establish some shared understanding about these behaviours by trying to define them. How easy or difficult is it to do this?

Once the behaviour has been effectively clarified, step two of the approach encourages you to consider what is causing the behaviours seen. Brownhill *et al.* (2006) provide a comprehensive list of reasons, some of which are identified below:

- Major life changes;
- Poor self esteem/self image;
- Lack of motivation or interest;
- Poor social/communication skills;
- Tiredness/exhaustion;
- Attitudes – personal, gender based;
- Illness and conditions – medical, biological, psychological, emotional and genetic;
- Attention seeking;
- High adrenaline/testosterone levels;
- Competition/rivalry;
- Home influences – culture, religious, parental expectations and viewpoints, socio-economic;
- Media influences – film, radio, TV, music, computer games, Internet images;
- Poor adjustment in the classroom;
- Poorly behaved role models – peers, parents, carers, guardians and teachers;
- Reactions to changes – temperature, smells, noise levels, space, weather;
- Testing the boundaries – assessing how far they can challenge the teacher;
- Traumatic family incidences – bereavement, serious illness, abuse, divorce, separation;
- Poor academic achievements;
- Stages of child development – age, sex, maturity, concentration levels, attention span;
- Inability to cope with one's own feelings and emotions;

- Peer group influences.

(Brownhill et al. 2006: 6. By kind permission of the
Continuum International Publishing Group)

Recognizing the impact of these influences on children's behaviour is a major factor in effective behaviour management. If you are unaware what is causing the behaviour then how can you put strategies in place to prevent the behaviour from escalating?

ACTIVITY

Select any two behaviours from either your personal list of behaviours or from the list on page X. Reflect on individual children either in your class or with whom you have worked and consider specific behaviours (either desirable or undesirable) they demonstrate. Record which of the influences presented above may have a potential impact on the behaviours exhibited by the children. We provide a completed example below to support you.

Name of child	Behaviour exhibited	Potential influences
Mark (5 years old)	Well mannered	<ul><li>Good role models – parents, grandparents, teacher</li><li>Responds well to praise when manners are commented on by staff members, including midday supervisors</li><li>Comes from a family with strong religious beliefs</li><li>Very nice, calm boy – seems to be an innate part of his general disposition</li></ul>

Once the specific influences have been identified, teachers are in a stronger position to select and adapt appropriate strategies which can be used to effectively manage these behaviours – this, in essence, forms the basis of step three of the 'be clear' approach. Many of the desirable behaviours identified in the list on pages 39 and 40 relate very much to learning and so it is our intention to examine these as a collection of behaviours which can be promoted through a set of effective and adaptable strategies.

> **NOTE**
>
> Strategies that you put into place need to continuously promote and reward the behaviours you expect – they will not just suddenly appear overnight. It is important to remember this when selecting and using strategies in the classroom.

To encourage the desirable behaviours from pages 39 and 40 you could:

1. offer generous specific praise to those who you see modelling behaviours you wish to see (Young 2005);
2. model behaviours you want to see so that children have something on which to base their own behaviours;
3. reward behaviours with a range of physical resources – stickers, stamps, treats (Canter and Canter 1992);
4. ensure peers and other adults, including the child's parents/carers, are made aware of the children's continuing achievements;
5. set children targets through verbal and written means to give direction towards their behavioural development;
6. offer a wealth of non-verbal recognition of the children's achievements and progress – a wink, a nod, a pat on the back, thumbs up, a smile (Kyriacou 2002);
7. encourage children to ask questions during your main teaching and during their own learning to help consolidate and extend thinking;
8. ensure tasks set are within the children's concentration spans;
9. allow children to work on tasks and activities in a variety of groupings;
10. ensure children engage with activities which play both to their strengths and areas for development;
11. use a variety of teaching resources and activities to hook children into their learning;
12. set extension tasks for children who need additional challenges and opportunities to learn;
13. ensure children's work from the whole class is clearly displayed around the classroom;
14. encourage children to be independent by assigning them specific jobs, training them to undertake certain duties to ensure the smooth running of the classroom.

In our eagerness to tackle poor behaviour head on there is a tendency for some of us to simply select and run with these strategies. However, we recommend that you reflect on the further considerations provided below for a number of strategies so that you are fully aware of the complexities of some of the ideas provided.

Strategy	Further considerations
1. Offer generous praise to those who you see modelling behaviours you wish to see	Ensure you remind children of the behaviours you want to see – how will they know what you want to see unless you tell them what you want to see? (Brownhill 2007)
	Do these behaviours have to come directly from you? It is interesting to ask children if they can tell you which behaviours they think you would like to see – most of the time they know how they should behave.
	When offering praise to children it is important to ensure you say the child's name so that they know it is being directed at them. Ensure the praise is also specific to the behaviour. Always ask yourself whether the child knows why they are getting the praise. If you are not clear about this then the child may be unsure how they can get further praise from you again.
4. Ensure peers and other adults, including the child's parents/carers, are made aware of the children's continuing achievements	It is good practice to share good behaviours with others. If communicating these with other children it can support them to see what they have to do to get into your good books. On the other hand, it may have the adverse effect of making others envious of the child receiving the praise, and this may cause hostility and possibly bullying if it is not dealt with sensitively.
	Parents and carers always like to hear good things about their children. Finding different ways to keep them informed of their children's behaviour is important. It is not always possible to speak to the parents and carers face to face due to work or other commitments, so consider making phone calls, writing letters or making notes in the children's reading record booklet to keep them up to date with their child's achievements. (Rogers, 2007)

One of the most interesting strategies offered is no. 6, which suggests you offer non-verbal recognition of the children's achievements and progress in the form of, for example, a wink, a nod, a pat on the back, thumbs up, or a smile. Some children, particularly those in Key Stage 2, may not want to receive their praise through verbal means as it may embarrass them, make them feel self-conscious or put them on the spot.

You should establish the most appropriate ways to give praise to each child in your class by either asking them or watching how they react when you give them praise in different ways. Non-verbal strategies can be a very effective way to pass on instant recognition to children about their behaviour without you having to use valuable learning and teaching time. Children are usually saturated with verbal messages, instructions and pieces of information at school every day so it is recommended that you work to ensure non-verbal strategies become an integral part of your 'silent yet successful' approach to behaviour management.

A touch of creativity, which fuels the content of Chapter 6, is needed to make strategy no. 9 work – 'allow children to work on tasks and activities in different groupings'.

ACTIVITY

How many different ways do you think it is possible to group children in school? Make a note of your creative ideas and compare them to the ideas presented below – how creative were you?

The whole idea of grouping children in different ways is to give them plenty of opportunities to mix with different children whilst building the personal and social skills they need to work effectively with others. Possible ways include:

- Individual
- Paired groupings
- Small groups (three/four)
- Half-class grouping
- Whole class
- Gender groups
- Mixed gender groups
- Ability groups
- Mixed-ability groups
- Age groupings
- Mixed ages
- Mixed key stages
- Mixed teacher
- Free-choice grouping
- Teacher/child-led
- Interest groups
- Talent groups
- Friendship groups

There are, however, potential issues which may stem from these grouping arrangements and result in behavioural difficulties. When grouping children of mixed abilities there is always the possibility that the lower-ability children will sit back and be led by the more able children, who in turn will become frustrated at the lack of effort or contributions the lower-ability children are making to proceedings. Friendship groups need to be carefully considered as sometimes the topic of conversation can veer dangerously from that stipulated by the teacher (Docking and McGrath 2002). Small groups are likely to be effective, yet you should consider who will be in each group so that you have a balance of leaders and followers. If all the leaders are grouped together, for example those children who will take charge and delegate roles and responsibilities to the rest of the group, then it is likely that arguments will erupt!

An interesting point of discussion focuses on strategy no. 13, which recommends that you 'ensure that children's work from the whole class is clearly displayed around the classroom'. All children like to see their work displayed as it helps to develop a sense of pride in their achievements. The difficulty with this is that sometimes there is not enough space to put up a piece of work from every child on the wall. Displays, however, do not always have to be on the wall – work hanging from 'washing lines' across the classroom, table-top displays, window-ledge displays, and 'anthologies' of children's work in the book corner are effective alternatives. It is recommended that you encourage children to help you in displaying their work, allow them to mount, label and position work as this will promote purposeful thinking skills to be developed and allow the children to take ownership of their classroom as, after all, it is theirs as much as yours. The way in which the classroom environment is arranged and presented has a direct impact on children's behaviour so encouraging the children to be organized and tidy will promote those positive behaviours you are striving to achieve (Cowley 2006).

Many of the undesirable behaviours identified on pages 39 and 40 relate heavily to the social skills of children, and it is this umbrella of behaviours which we will examine next. The importance of children being able to engage appropriately with their peers and other adults cannot be underestimated. These behaviours can affect the quality of learning and teaching which takes place in the classroom, and make it very difficult for you to work with members of your class when their basic social skills prevent them for building effective working relationships with others. Suggested strategies to manage these undesirable behaviours include the following:

a) Model behaviours you would like to see in your class – let them see the behaviours in practice.
b) Try strategically ignoring the behaviours seen (Glenn *et al.* 2004).
c) Use personal, social, health and citizenship education (PSHCE) and circle time opportunities to discuss undesirable behaviours, establishing strategies to turn the negatives into positives.
d) Praise children when you see behaviours you want to see being demonstrated (Cohen *et al.* 2004).
e) Empathize with the child if something in their home life is causing them to behave inappropriately, but make it clear that their behaviour is unacceptable.
f) Distract the child with stimulating activities and resources.
g) Talk to parents and carers about the behaviours you are seeing in class – work together to ensure these behaviours are eradicated with speed and efficiency (see Chapter 8 for further information).
h) Use stories, music, drama and dance as creative mediums to explore behaviours and the effects they can have on others (see Chapter 7 for further information).
i) Use your 'teacher glare' to raise awareness of your dislike of behaviours children are exhibiting.
j) Use 'time out' as a strategy to give the child some time to consider what they have done and how they might be able to rectify issues and incidences which have occurred.
k) Plan for active and energetic learning in the class to prevent children becoming

bored, impatient and irritable. Ensure there are plenty of resources for children to use so they are not forced to hang around waiting to use them.

Again, certain strategies detailed above need to be examined in greater depth to appreciate the complexities of some of the ideas presented.

Strategy	Further considerations
b) Try strategically ignoring the behaviours seen	Sometimes, if the behaviour is not too severe, it is better to simply ignore it as many children simply demonstrate such behaviours to get some sort of reaction from you, be it negative or positive. If children know you will not react, most will stop doing it. Others, however, will continue – you just have to know which children are likely to do so.
e) Empathize with the child if something in their home life is causing them to behave inappropriately, but make it clear that that their behaviour is unacceptable	Knowing what is going on in the child's life outside of school can be a very useful way of establishing what sort of day you are likely to have with particular individuals in your class. This does not mean that you have to ask every child in your class what is going on at home as you could be there for a number of hours having to deal with trivial issues, or have parents and carers complaining that you are prying into their private lives. Instead, ask general questions about how things are going and speak to other teachers in the school who have siblings in their classes as they may be aware of issues. Speaking to parents and carers when an incident has occurred may help to shed a little light on the situation. However, take care; you are not a trained counsellor.

Many of you will be familiar with the use of time out (strategy j) as a valuable approach to managing behaviour, for it quickly gives teachers the opportunity to move disruptive children from particular incidences whilst still managing the behaviour of the rest of the class. Having a time-out chair is useful as long as it is in the teacher's eye line – leaving a child on the chair for an entire lesson is not appropriate as they will miss valuable learning and teaching time and will undoubtedly forget to reflect properly on what they have done. A sand timer might be a useful resource to indicate the amount of time a child needs to stay on the chair. Always ensure the child is given the opportunity to tell you what happened after the incident and that you give a little time to reiterating expectations of behaviour to ensure further incidences do not replicate themselves.

EXTENDING YOUR LEARNING

For those of you interested in furthering your understanding of the different types of time out and the complexities of overcoming some of the practical difficulties associated with it, you are encouraged to engage with the following readings:

Kerr, M.M. and Nelson, C.M. (2006) *Strategies for Addressing Behaviour Problems in the Classroom,* 5th edition. Upper Saddle River, NJ: Pearson Merrill Prentice Hall.

Rogers, B. (2002) *Classroom Behaviour: A Practical Guide to Teaching, Behaviour Management and Colleague Support,* 2nd edition. London: Paul Chapman.

REFLECT

- What have you learned from the strategies and the further considerations/analysis provided in this chapter so far?
- Which strategies do you intend to adopt as your own practice? Why are you now thinking in this way?
- Consider which strategies you are reticent to use – why do you consider these strategies not to be appropriate? How could you adapt these strategies so that they are more in line with your way of thinking?

The notion of 'tips for teachers' or simple 'tricks of the trade' is an expected yet controversial aspect of any book about behaviour management because many educationalists, including Porter (2007), argue that just giving teachers a 'sea of strategies' undermines the value of critical thinking, theory and reflective practice. The concern is that these strategies can only take you so far – if these are all you have to fight poor behaviour and none of them work, what do you do then? We are of the view, however, that offering some ideas is a useful way to initially support teachers because it is likely that you will encounter a specific behaviour, apply strategies recommended to you and they do not work. If this occurs consider the following:

Top Tips

TOP TIPS!

- Use humour where appropriate.
- Avoid empty threats.
- Remain calm.
- Avoid crying in front of the children.

- Stress to the child that it is their behaviour you disapprove of, not them personally.
- Avoid taking your anger out on the children.
- Gain control as quickly as you can.
- Avoid holding a grudge.
- Give children a choice – either X or Y.
- Avoid grabbing or smacking a child.
- Look for someone who is behaving well.
- Clearly state what you expect to see in the child.
- Avoid comparing children to others.
- Use your voice effectively – try not to raise your voice.

Many teachers feel relatively confident in using strategies like those suggested above to manage the day-to-day behaviours exhibited by children in their classrooms, yet seem under-prepared to effectively manage behaviours exhibited by children who have special educational needs. It is important that we consider this as the next part of this chapter.

Behaviours associated with children who have special educational needs (SEN) common to the primary classroom

It is inevitable that you will encounter children in your classroom who have special educational needs. With inclusion a high priority for every school across Britain, teachers are keen to develop effective strategies, techniques and approaches to support these children, whilst ensuring that any behaviours, which are a result of their needs, do not hinder their own or other's progress, or the ability of the teacher to actually teach them.

ACTIVITY

Consider the kinds of behaviours children may exhibit which you would have to manage and record these for your personal reference.

Special educational need	Behaviours exhibited
Dyspraxia	
Autistic tendencies	
Gifted children	

Tourette's syndrome
Selective mutism
Asperger's syndrome
Attention deficit hyperactivity disorder
Physical impairments

Your initial reactions to reflecting on the content of this table are likely to vary. Some of you may be frightened about the prospect of managing children with these needs, whilst others are apprehensive because you do not know what these conditions actually are, what causes them, what behaviours children who have them exhibit, or how they can effectively manage them. Do not worry. Every teacher has at one time or another had feelings like these – it is perfectly normal. What is important is that as a professional you act positively to overcome these apprehensions. One way to do this is to find out some answers so let us begin by considering what these needs actually are.

ACTIVITY

Draw a line to link the conditions with their appropriate definitions. Alternatively, make a note of your 'letter pairs' on a separate piece of paper.

Condition	Definition
A. Dyspraxia is . . .	Z. a neurological disorder which affects the ability of children to have appropriate social relationships with others.
B. Autistic tendencies are . . .	Y. those who have skills, capabilities or knowledge which exceed those of children of a similar age.
C. Gifted children are . . .	X. a complex anxiety disorder characterized by a child's lack of speech in one or more social contexts.

D. Tourette's syndrome is …	W. include children who have mobility difficulties due to a lack of formed limbs or medical conditions including muscular dystrophy and spina bifida.
E. Selective mutism is …	V. an inherited neurological disorder characterized by involuntary body movements and uncontrollable vocalizations known as 'tics'
F. Asperger's syndrome is…	U. a worrying blend of children being impulsive, lacking in inhibition and concentration and having poor social skills.
G. Attention deficit hyperactivity disorder is…	T. an impairment or immaturity in the organization of movement, language, perception and thought.
H. Physical impairments are…	S. usually characterized by a rigidity of thought and behaviour, limited/impaired verbal and non-verbal communication, and difficulty with social relationships and interactions.

Answers can be found at the end of this chapter (page 62).

The purpose of this activity is to help you distinguish between the different conditions and give you some ideas with regard to the kind of behaviours associated with each one. As each special need is different it is not easy to highlight common behaviours between all of the conditions. Instead, it is more beneficial to indicate specific behaviours which separate some of the key conditions from others.

Condition	Examples of specific behaviours
Dyspraxia	Poor balance and hand–eye co-ordination, unclear speech, poor memory, tendency to fall, trip or bump into things
Autistic tendencies	Preoccupation with objects and repetitive movements, anxiety when experiencing change in routines, distortion in movements, unawareness of personal identity, impairments in interpersonal relationships
Tourette's syndrome	Involuntary body movements, uncontrollable vocalizations, outbursts of swearing
Selective mutism	Little eye contact with others, lips tightly sealed, standing/sitting motionless, biting lips, seeming to ignore others
Asperger's syndrome	Talking non-stop, showing little empathy for others, inability to take turns, poor attention span, dominating conversations, blatantly truthful

ADHD	Not paying attention to details, making careless mistakes, poor concentration level, losing things, fidgeting, talking excessively, interrupting others

REFLECT

- How do the details presented above compare with the thoughts you were invited to consider at the start of this section on behaviours associated with SEN?
- How do they support, extend or challenge your thinking?

The details in the table above are designed to give you an overview of the kinds of behaviour exhibited by children with these conditions – it is not designed to be a tool which can be used to assess children against. To ensure a more rigorous approach is taken to the diagnosis of SEN, a number of different specialists need to be consulted. These include:

- occupational therapists;
- speech and language therapists;
- psychologists;
- a general practitioner (GP).

For further information linked to this you are encouraged to engage with Chapter 8, which not only examines the work of some of these specialists but also discusses ways of initiating and sustaining partnerships with them.

Our next consideration focuses on what can be done to manage these behaviours. The case study and reflection below are designed to highlight the potential effects of selecting inappropriate management strategies.

CASE STUDY

James, a 5-year-old with Asperger's syndrome, found it very difficult to co-operate and participate with others when group work was planned for the class to undertake. James's teacher found him to be rather 'self-centred' and 'unmanageable' but she also felt quite sorry for him and therefore planned to always work with him on a one-to-one basis so that he completed his work and felt supported in the classroom.

REFLECTION

- What do you think about the practice detailed above?
- Do you think it is appropriate for the teacher to feel sorry for James? If so, why? If not, why not?
- What do you think the potential outcomes of this practice are for James? What about James's teacher? James's peers? James's next teacher?

Whilst there is a tendency for teachers and children to sometimes overlook behaviours exhibited by those with special educational needs, it is important not to take pity on them or let these children get away with inappropriate behaviours to the detriment of lowering standards in behaviour, learning and expectations. Offering support to these children is important, yet it needs to be in moderation compared to the needs of the rest of the class as focusing your attention on one child is not an effective use of your time. You will find a number of strategies below in addition to those already presented in this chapter to aid your work with children with SEN. A number of these strategies can be applied to all of the needs discussed:

- Avoid shouting at the child – it is not necessarily their fault that certain behaviours are being exhibited.
- Be patient with the child.
- Differentiate work set for the child to ensure they can achieve, irrespective of the levels of attainment of the other children in the class.
- Set realistic targets and expectations for work and behaviour – clearly agree, display and review these (Emmerson 2001).
- Work with specialist support to devise and implement strategies and programmes to build on skills and achievements.
- Keep instructions clear and to the point (McSherry 2001).
- Plan for short bursts of activity to grab and sustain their levels of attention.
- Praise the child as and when appropriate to maintain/raise levels of self esteem (DfES 2001).
- Maintain an open dialogue with parents and carers so that good practice can be shared between home and school.
- Ensure that the work children engage with caters for their learning needs.

Now that you are equipped with some of the tools of the behaviour management trade, let us put them to the notional test by examining an incident involving a child with a behavioural condition.

SCENARIO

A child with Tourette's syndrome is making body movements and vocalizations which are disturbing others on the table at which the child is sitting. What would you do?

1.   Play calming music in the background?
2.   Allow the child to have some time out?
3.   Use additional adult support to help the child?
4.   Move the child so that they do not distract others?
5.   Firmly ask the child to stop being silly?
6.   Ignore the behaviour, telling the children on the table to ignore it too?

Those strategies numbered 1–3 are useful for managing the behaviour of a child with Tourette's syndrome as their 'tics' are often made worse when the child is stressed, tired or anxious. Such strategies may alleviate some of the discomfort the child is feeling. Strategy 4 has positive and negative attributes as, on the one hand, it would certainly allow the rest of the table to focus on their work but, on the other, it would potentially ostracize the child with Tourette's syndrome, making others in the class think that the child had done something wrong. Strategy 5 is a rather inappropriate strategy to adopt: asking children to suppress their tics is like asking us to hold back a sneeze – the effort required to do this is enormous. Strategy 6 is useful in that it may help to reduce the likelihood of children with Tourette's syndrome becoming the butt of children's jokes or being bullied or labelled as some kind of 'freak' if it is considered to be a normal occurrence. This obviously depends on the severity of the tics being displayed; it may be that the child requires some form of medication or behavioural therapy to help manage their tics. This level of analysis should allow you to critically consider your actions and make you aware that your choices of management strategies have direct consequences on children's behaviour, some of which may be positive, whilst others may not be so positive. Reflect on the strategies suggested for the next scenario.

SCENARIO

A child who has selective mutism suddenly freezes whilst reading her home/school reading book to you. What would you do?

- Encourage the child to continue reading?
- Raise your voice – the child is clearly wasting your time?
- Sigh and patiently wait?
- Reassure the child, offering them support to overcome their feelings of anxiety e.g. 'Breathe deeply!' 'Take your time!'?
- Bribe the child with a sweet or extra playtime if they will continue to read?

- Let the child do something different and come back to reading later on?
- Ask the child to read to another adult – parent helper or teaching assistant?
- Ensure you let the child know that you recognize they are scared and that you are there for them? (Tilstone and Rose 2003)
- Send the book back home with the child – they clearly cannot read every word?

Clearly those strategies which comfort and support or encourage the child are more appropriate than those which dismiss the child's behaviour and are rather reactionary in nature. Reflecting back on our 'be clear' approach to behaviour management (Figure 1), knowing why the child suddenly 'freezes' up is the second step to effectively managing the behaviour – is the book too easy? Too hard? Are they stressed or tired? Do they not like the person they are reading to? Are there home influences which are causing this behaviour? There are, of course, other reasons not detailed above which cause selective mutism and you are encouraged to undertake an internet search for three websites which detail more reasons to support and extend your knowledge base.

REFLECT

By adopting the same analytical approach to the scenarios presented above, consider what strategies you would put in place to manage the behaviours exhibited below.

(A) A young girl is being given instructions linked to the creative design and technology task she is to undertake in a few moments' time. She has ADHD and shows many of the behaviours detailed on page 52. What would you do?
(B) A boy in your class is undertaking gymnastics in the hall with all of the large apparatus out. He has Asperger's syndrome and is struggling to meet the objective set by you for the class. What would you do?
(C) A girl in your class has diagnosed autism. The school is undertaking a planned fire drill at 11 a.m. The girl feels very secure with the routines which are followed in class and can become volatile when things are changed which upsets many of the other children in the class. What would you do?

Whilst there may only be a handful of children in your class who have special educational needs there is one aspect of school life for all children which inevitably has the potential to bring with it behaviour difficulties – transitions.

Behaviours associated with transitions

Every year children in our schools move up, either within the key stages – Year 1 into Year 2, and Year 4 into Year 5 – or between the key stages – Early Years Foundation Stage into Key Stage 1, Key Stage 1 into Key Stage 2, and Key Stage 2 into Key Stage 3. We shall refer to these moves as transition points and consider the implications of transition points between the key stages to begin with.

For both the children and their parents, moving between the different key stages can be an anxious time as it is clearly indicates a change in the demands expected of them, particularly with reference to the amount and challenge of the content of work set and raised expectations relating to their behaviour. For children approaching these transition points it is understandable that children may experience feelings of discomfort, nervousness, and anxiety because each point highlights a new stage in their education which may bring with it a few sleepless nights. Of course, not all children suffer anxiety, often feeling excited about the prospective changes. Children will usually have a lot of questions at this time: what is my new teacher going to be like? Where will my coat peg be? Where will I sit in class? Will I be sitting next to my best friend? What if my new teacher shouts a lot? Will the work be too difficult? As a result, children's behaviour can change in a number of ways – some children act very confidently and give the impression that they are not scared of the change, overcompensating for their underlying anxieties by using excessive bravado and becoming rather arrogant and dismissive. Others may regress into themselves, becoming very quiet and potentially tearful at the thought of the imminent move. This is particularly likely when children move from Year 6 into Year 7 – many consider themselves to be 'top dog' in primary school because they are in their final year but then suddenly find themselves in a new situation which may lead to feelings of inadequacy when they enter secondary school. It is therefore inevitable that they will feel confused or threatened by this move. So how can you ensure the transitions between the key stages do not present any adverse behavioural difficulties?

Top Tips

TOP TIPS!

- Plan sessions for the new teachers to come into class and work with the children to build up relationships. Team-teach with colleagues over a number of weeks before giving them the opportunity to work with the class on their own.
- Give children the opportunity to visit their new classroom so that they can familiarize themselves with the new environment.
- Plan whole-school mornings/days which allow children to move up to their new classes.
- Ensure children coming into your class are aware of your expectations before they move classes – use circle time opportunities to share your thoughts, feelings and ideas about behaviour so that the children are clear about who you are and what you will and will not stand for.

> Discuss the similarities and differences between your expectations and those of previous teachers.
> - Encourage the children to talk with members of your current class so that they can get a true picture of what you are like. You may encourage buddy writing pairs between classes of older children.
> - Write a letter or create a PowerPoint presentation with audio and video footage to share with the children about you and your teaching. Alternatively, get the children in your class to do it for you.

Whilst this supports the children, it is important for the parents to be considered – do remember that they will be anxious too. Ways to offer this support include the following:

- Send a letter to the parents introducing yourself and addressing some of their likely concerns.
- Encourage parents of your current class to talk to the parents of children moving up in September.
- Adopt an open-door policy allowing parents to come in to see you teach or set aside times before, during or after school when you can speak with individuals or groups of parents about their children coming into your class.
- Organize a parents' evening where you can talk to the parents as a whole group and answer questions.
- Use the school's website to answer frequently asked questions by parents.
- Empathize with them – their experiences of school may not have been positive, so assure them you will make it positive for their children.

Interestingly, and yet not surprisingly, many of the strategies and suggestions offered above are easily transferable and adaptable to manage the behaviours of children as they move within the key stage into different classes at the start of the school year. Preparation is the key to ensuring transitions are effective. Planning exciting and educationally stimulating activities for the children in the first few weeks also helps to prevent behavioural difficulties from developing.

An aspect of transitions which is sometimes overlooked, yet which we feel is important to examine, is linked to the notion of transitions between activities and practitioners during a school day – for example, the main class teacher undertaking their planning, preparation and assessment time (PPA) whilst a higher level teaching assistant (HLTA) takes over the teaching of the whole class. It is interesting to note that OFSTED (2007) continue to comment on this aspect of practice in the classroom, highlighting how poor transitions in lessons result in many unnecessary behavioural difficulties occurring.

Let us initially look at transitions between activities. Most teachers are likely to structure their lessons in small bites so that there are usually some opportunities to get ready and review previous learning, some direct taught input, time for the children to engage in small-group and individual work, and an opportunity for the class to come together to review learning. Even though the naming of each section is different, this structure can be applied to a numeracy session or to a gymnastics lesson, as shown in the table below:

Aspects of taught sessions	Numeracy session	Gymnastics lesson
'Getting ready' and reviewing previous learning	Oral mental starter	Warm up
Direct taught input	Main teaching exposition	Direct teaching – floor work
Small-group/individual learning opportunities	Group/individual tasks	Apparatus opportunities
Whole-class review of learning	Plenary	Review and cool down

By planning in this way teachers aim to maintain the interest of the children they teach, delivering in bursts to ensure progression in sessions and develop concentration and interactivity levels. However, if the transitions between these sections are not smooth or well planned it is likely that children, irrespective of their age, will behave in any of the following ways:

- quickly become off task;
- become restless and bored;
- unnecessarily talk amongst themselves;
- become noisy through laughter;
- poke and prod other children with their fingers and feet;
- wriggle about on the carpet.

Why might these transitions not be smooth? Reflect critically on the scenario below, highlighting aspects of practice which you feel contribute to the poor transitions in the lesson.

SCENARIO

Miss Fisher is teaching a science lesson to her Year 2 class and notices that they are becoming slightly restless on the carpet. Looking at her watch, Miss Fisher realizes that she has been talking for nearly 25 minutes. In less than one minute she quickly runs through what she wants the children to do and then says 'OK! Off you go!'

It seems to take for ever for the children to sit down at their desks, and when they do settle they have sat in the wrong places. The noise level in the classroom rises considerably as Miss Fisher quickly gathers together the resources needed for the children to do the experiment. Miss Fisher is unable to lower the children's voices with any real effect as she rushes

> around the classroom, answering questions which the second-year B.Ed.
> student on placement with her has about her supporting role with the
> lower-ability group.

It is likely you identified the following:

- The teacher runs over in terms of the main taught input – there is too much talking and not enough doing.
- Resources are not ready for the children to use when they get to their tables.
- The children do not know where they have to go or what they have to do when they are sent to do their group tasks – they have not had the opportunity to ask any questions or check anything before they are set to task.
- The student teacher supporting the lower-ability group appears not to be fully prepared and is unclear about what the children have to do. Unfortunately this clarification takes place when they should have been leading and supporting the children.
- The children waste valuable learning and teaching time by not getting to their tables in a suitable amount of time – the notion of dawdling is evidently clear.

Whilst it is easy to be critical of others' practice, in order for transitions to be smooth and effective there are a number of simple strategies to prevent behavioural difficulties like those in the scenario above from occurring:

- Ensure you have spoken to any adult supporting group activities before the lesson. Provide them with a written structure or plan of what you want them to do and the kind of work/progress you expect the children to produce/make. Encourage them to ask any questions before the children begin the lesson.
- Only send one group of children off to their respective tasks when you are certain the children know what they have to do. Be clear about which part of the classroom you expect the children to work in before they move.
- Provide instructions on cards for those children who are able to read/ comprehend them, as opposed to always having to verbally instruct them to save learning and teaching time.
- Establish your expectations of what you want the children to do when they leave the carpet and how they are to do it – identify children who model those behaviours you like as and when these are demonstrated.
- Set time limits (Visser 2000). Use a one-minute sand timer to visually indicate the amount of time children have to get to their tables and settle into their work.
- Keep an eye on the amount of time you use for your main teaching – work to ensure that you do not overrun. Have a large clock in your eyesight or ask your assistant to indicate to you when it is time to move on.
- Ensure all resources are ready and set out on the tables before the children move to the activity. If you are trying to promote independence, ensure individuals are

given specific jobs (distributing the pencils, handing out the books) and assess how effectively and quickly these are undertaken.

Let us now consider the transitions which occur between practitioners during the school day. Children will come into contact with a number of different adults who will either be teaching them or supporting them pastorally. It is important that transitions between these adults are fluid, well planned and calm to prevent behavioural difficulties from occurring. There are various strategies to ensure this:

- Ensure children are ready for the handover before it actually takes place so that you are not rushed or flustered if adults arrive early or late.
- Remind children of your expectations of their behaviour when they go to another practitioner. Ask practitioners to repeat/remind children of these expectations before they start teaching to secure understanding.
- Develop strategies to pass on information which will not interfere with transitions. Ask teaching assistants to pass information on verbally a couple of minutes before you hand your class to the midday supervisor. Ask midday supervisors to make a note of good/poor behaviours in a little book which can be looked at by the teacher or teaching assistant during afternoon registration, as opposed to having a lengthy chat when the children are in class.
- Avoid leaving the children until they are settled and the practitioner in charge is happy for you to go.
- Work with other practitioners to ensure they are happy with what they are doing and that they have everything they need to teach the children prior to the teaching actually taking place.
- Follow up poor behaviour in collaboration with other practitioners.

One final aspect of transitions which we will examine looks at transitions which occur when children move between different schools. Whilst this may only apply to one or two children in your class over the year, it is important to be aware of behavioural difficulties which may result from this move. Having some understanding of the reasoning behind these departures/arrivals will help you to appreciate the complexities of the situation and thus provide you with a knowledge base to ensure you support the children and parents involved in the best way that you can. For example, some children may leave the school as one of their parents has received a job promotion which involves relocation. On the other hand, children moving as a result of their parents separating may exhibit difficult behaviours – crying, depression, temper tantrums – for the teacher to have to manage.

For those children leaving you we suggest you do the following:

- Encourage the child to see it as a positive experience – use circle time opportunities to talk about the exciting times ahead whilst acknowledging their feelings of apprehension about the move. Support the child in managing these feelings as and when they are experienced yet continue to have high expectations of their behaviour.
- Ask the rest of the class to spend as much time as they can with their friend to make their last few weeks as exciting and positive as possible.

- Invite the child to have some quality one-to-one time with you if required for them to talk through their feelings and thoughts.
- Work with the parents to ensure all paperwork is completed relating to the child's departure.
- Ensure that you have completed any documentation required by the new school and send to them reports and workbooks to establish levels of attainment across the curriculum.
- Use e-mails or letters from the children to contact the child a couple of weeks after their move to see how they are.

For children coming to you from another school we recommend you do the following:

- Ensure you have thoroughly read the induction policy of the school so you are aware of effective protocol and practices (Hook and Vass 2000).
- If at all possible, send letters or e-mails to the new child with drawings of the class and staff members so that they can put a name to the different faces they will meet.
- Plan time to talk to parents and children prior to starting if at all possible to answer any queries and establish your expectations of working and behaviour.
- Contact the child's previous school to ask for school reports and workbooks so that you can establish areas of strength and weakness in the child's attainment and plan for them accordingly.
- Use circle time opportunities to welcome the child into class.
- Identify children to sit with and work with the new child to build relationships. Encourage the class to invite the new child to play with them during playtimes.

It is hoped that using these kinds of strategies will help to alleviate some of the behavioural issues which stem from transitions, in whichever form they appear, and ensure quality learning and teaching in your classroom.

> **KEY POINTS**
>
> - Adopt the three-step 'be clear' approach to effective behaviour management (see Figure 1).
> - Focus more on the desirable behaviours in children as opposed to those which are undesirable.
> - Take care with the kind of terminology you use to describe behaviours.
> - Adapt strategies so that they are appropriate for the behaviour and the child.
> - Avoid thinking negatively about behaviours associated with SEN.
> - Be aware of the different transitions in children's lives, planning for them appropriately.

ACTIVITY ANSWERS (see page 51)

You should have made the following links: A–T, B–S, C–Y, D–V, E–X, F–Z, G–U, H–W.

4 Behaviour management and emotional intelligence

This chapter focuses on the ways in which we can help children to understand their identity, feelings and responses to others. It will specifically examine:

- definitions of emotional intelligence and emotional literacy;
- how these link to children's emotional growth;
- how children learn to understand themselves;
- what we can do in the classroom to ensure our learners' affective development is carefully nurtured.

Emotional intelligence

In the classroom we constantly strive to build and develop the cognitive domain. There can be little question that most of us do this well and that the children we teach, learn the basics and much more besides in preparation for their secondary education. 'Emotional intelligence' is a term we frequently hear people use in educational settings, but what does it mean? Emotional intelligence, or 'emotional literacy' as it is sometimes called, refers to the affective domain, the dimension of self that is associated with feelings.

> The tendency to separate the cognitive from the affective is reflected in our separation of the mind from the body, of thinking from feeling, and the way we have dichotomized the work of the head from the work of the hand.
>
> (Eisner 1982: 30)

Many teachers and parents see education as preparation for a child's future life, to enable them to live and work in the community. What we often forget, however, is the fact that all children are living in the world *now*. They need nurturing to enable them to live from day to day as they grow up in their community. Providing opportunities to develop the affective domain is essential in this growth.

'Emotions are states of mind that arise as a result of specific experiences and drive us to take action' (Maines 2003: 8). They cannot be seen, although when we experience an emotion it is often reflected in a facial expression, gesture, body language or verbal action. Baron-Cohen and Maines (2003) agree that there is skill involved in reading human emotion, and that it is an important aspect of human development. We explore this later in this chapter. Let us begin by considering what we mean by emotional intelligence and how it differs from emotional literacy.

Research suggests that emotional intelligence and emotional literacy are two quite separate entities (Matthews 2006). Mayer and Salovey (1997: 10), quoted in Matthews (2006: 37), define emotional intelligence as:

> the ability to perceive accurately, appraise and express emotion; the ability to access and/or generate feelings which facilitate thought; the ability to understand emotion and emotional knowledge; the ability to regulate emotions to promote emotional and intellectual growth.

Steiner (1997: 11), quoted in Matthews (2006: 43), provides the following definition of emotional literacy:

> the ability to understand your emotions, the ability to listen to others and empathise with their emotions, and the ability to express emotions productively.

REFLECT

What do these definitions mean to you? How do they fit with your perspectives and experiences? Think for a moment about how you feel connected to your own emotions. Perhaps there are times when you feel more connected than others. How well do you think you understand yourself? In what ways are you able to apply strategies to deal with certain emotions? It is worth remembering that sometimes both negative and positive feelings can evoke inappropriate responses.

Using the grid below consider your responses and strategies for coping with your feelings.

Emotion	Response	Strategy
Unhappiness		
Anger		

Elation
_____

Boredom
_____

Frustration
_____

Stress
_____

Anxiety
_____

Excitement
_____

Concern
_____

Aggravation
_____

Disappointment
_____

Anticipation

These definitions provide us with two different perspectives. In the former we are considering the idea of the ability to understand our own feelings, whereas the latter takes us a step further by considering understanding ourselves and how we understand other people. How many of the emotions listed above are ones that present themselves because of other people or our feelings towards them?

For us to work effectively in the classroom we need to be aware of both of these factors. It is essential that in order to understand others, we must first understand ourselves and be aware of how we respond and react to our own emotions in any given situation. We should therefore be mindful that these two terms are quite different in themselves but that they are intrinsically linked in developing a person in a holistic way.

In their model of emotional intelligence, Boyatzis and Burckle (1999) consider six critical core 'stabilities' involved in cognitive and emotional development that link to performance:

- emotional self-awareness;
- accurate self-awareness;

- self-confidence;
- emotional self-control,
- empathy,
- influence.

They suggest that the fundamental stability here is self-awareness. Being self-aware means that you can see yourself as others see you. This requires the ability to understand who you are as a person and to recognize your positive traits as well as less positive traits. Once we are well acquainted with who we are, we can start to consider the impact we have on others, the way in which we present our body language, our spoken language and ourselves. All of these are important aspects in forming relationships that are healthy and stable.

Next time you are faced with a difficult situation, ask yourself the following questions:

- What do I know about this child?
- Do I know all the facts of the situation?
- Am I in control of the situation?
- Do I need assistance?
- Am I applying school policy to the incident?
- Am I at eye level with the child?
- Is the child looking at me?
- Am I calm?
- Is the child calm enough to talk to me and listen to me?
- Am I being fair?

It is important that we assess our own belief system about the children we teach. What preconceived ideas do we bring to the classroom? What are our expectations for our pupils? Do we bring biases to the classroom? Are we wiling to rethink these to form positive relationships and ensure that all children achieve and learn at a higher level?

Following on from this, let us consider how we deal with our own emotional responses when we are dealing with children's behaviour. Are there underlying factors that affect the way in which we handle behaviour in school? By reflecting on our own ability to manage our affective responses, we can help young people do the same.

We know that children sometimes behave inappropriately, but then we too can have challenging days and our responses may not always be appropriate either.

SCENARIO

It's a really busy time of year. I have 36 reports to write, an immense pile of marking to do and the children are starting to misbehave in class. Next week is Arts Week and I just don't think I can get through the week without losing my temper. I feel physically exhausted and every day feels like a chore. We normally have a lovely time together, but right now I am finding it very difficult to cope.

Every week is hectic in the school calendar, but some weeks are more hectic than others. Look at the practical advice below to see which of the strategies you might consider adopting to help you through the pinch points.

Top Tips

TOP TIPS!		
• Give yourself time to do some exercise. A brisk walk, a short run or an exercise class will make you feel better.	• Change your plans. If you do not think you can cope with what you have planned for today you can always do it tomorrow.	• Confide in a colleague or a friend – a trouble shared is a trouble halved. You might find they are feeling the same way.
• If you feel anxious in class, stop the lesson and bring everybody to the carpet for some quiet time.	• Tell some jokes, ask the children to tell you some jokes – but make sure you pick your jokers carefully.	• If you cannot confide in someone, write down your worries. It helps just to get it off your chest.
• Have a sing-song in class. Sing a nonsense song or a favourite class song and get everybody to join in.	• Try going into role, forget your worries for a short time and be Henry VIII or Florence Nightingale.	• Make a note of the busy times and plan for the pressure points.

Source: Adapted from Brownhill *et al*. (2006).

By being aware of how we feel we can prevent ourselves from taking out our stresses and strains on the children. It is not always their fault and we should remember this. We should model the behaviour we expect from our pupils, so by remaining calm, consistent in our message and emphasizing the positive aspects of the situation/child we can help children to behave in the way we expect. Looking after our physical and emotional well-being is essential – a 'healthy mind in a healthy body'. By doing so we can approach difficult situations in a rational, composed manner.

Positive relationships

Developing good relationships is essential if we are to succeed in managing behaviour and expectations consistently and effectively. Knowing the children we teach on a more personal level promotes harmony and enables expectations to remain balanced. How might we enable these positive relationships to flourish? We can approach this in a number of ways. Research (Roffey 2007) suggests that by taking account of both our own emotions and those of our pupils we can take steps to make each day more rewarding for children and teachers alike. But how might we do this?

CONSIDERATION

With a colleague or fellow student, discuss ways in which you might develop a range of strategies for getting to know children in your class and for developing positive relationships. Compare them with the list below. How many did you match, how many more did you find?

- Get to know all pupils by name.

- Greet children in the morning, after playtime, lunchtime. Use a smile, a nod and a wink for positive reinforcement.

- Have a special chair for children to sit on in the classroom if they feel they need some individual time with you.

- Find out pupils' interests and plan them into classroom activities.

- Provide talking and listening opportunities within the school day for children to express themselves.

- Find qualities to like and admire in the children and talk about this with them.

- Talk to children about their home life, pets, hobbies, weekend or holiday.

- Provide positive feedback during independent and group work to scaffold learning and build feelings of self-efficacy and self-esteem.

- Ask the children to bring in a special object from home and to talk about why they value it.

Every day children have to deal with experiences and problems before they even come to school. These external factors can influence the way that children behave in the classroom, their emotions and ability to deal with them can play a large part in the behaviour they display.

There are children who are reluctant to leave their parents, children who behave inappropriately the moment they enter the classroom and those who physically and mentally abuse their peers and teachers. Their feelings of anxiety and emotional distress can present themselves in negative ways. These children are not to blame for their behaviour. They are already dealing with a range of experiences that they often have no control over and their behaviour in school can be one way in which they are able to externalize their feelings.

> Emotions are an integral component of individual constructs. Anxiety and depression are often masked as defiance. As an 'externalising behaviour', this is more likely to take up the available attention. By contrast, the sadness underlying fury may not be considered important, as it is not something that needs to be 'managed'.
>
> (Roffey 2007)

Pupils in school link their feelings to the expectations presented to them by teachers. This is inextricably linked to self-efficacy – the knowledge that you can achieve enables you to achieve again. Once a pupil feels a failure in a curriculum area they are likely to feel challenged and anxious about approaching work related to that subject. If they feel they will fail on a task they may display behaviour that we perceive as inappropriate. Recognizing these emotions and responding to them is fundamental for achieving a good work ethic in the classroom. Knowing pupils well and ensuring that work is matched appropriately to their needs is the way to ensure effective teaching and learning – and we owe that much to those in our care.

Of course, not only children experience these feelings; we too can feel threatened and challenged in the classroom. We may feel that our own subject knowledge is not adequate for a teaching session and the way in which we behave can have a direct influence on pupil behaviour as a result. Being on top of material is essential if we are to feel secure and confident in our teaching ability.

ACTIVITY

Consider the ways in which you can ensure that both you and the young people you teach can feel secure and confident in intellectual abilities. Link these to feelings, teaching and learning.

Feelings	
You	They

Learning	
You	They

Teaching	
You	They

A strategy is only as good as the context in which it is embedded – and relationships are the most significant factor in determining success (Roffey 2007). Do your strategies and ideas enable the relationships to be genuine and sound? Some days are more difficult than others, and children can push the boundaries in the hope of getting a reaction or attention. If we recognize both their emotional state of mind and our own, we are well on the way to building those secure relationships in which everybody is valued, as are their contributions and their ideas. We may need to pay extra attention to our responses and reactions in certain situations and on certain days to ensure that we are fair, consistent and calm in the way we deal with particular children.

Look at a few of the ideas we had in relation to securing quality teaching and learning. It is not solely a matter of how we deal with situations but also how we present ideas and concepts: how we listen to and value responses, how we take pupil needs into consideration when planning, delivering and assessing lesson content. How do your ideas compare with the ones below?

You	They
Feelings	
Get a good night's sleep – feeling tired exacerbates irritability and makes it difficult for us to make good judgements in the classroom.	Allow for pupils who are tired – they may not have slept due to disturbances at home. Use circle time in the morning as a greeting to start the day in a positive way.
Start the day off with a smile and some special time with the class. This enables everybody to feel that they have the same starting point for the day.	Give all children the opportunity to feel involved and included in the 'sharing' time. Use your 'star chair' or 'champion's cushion' to bolster those who need to feel secure.
Look out for good behaviour and reward it immediately. You will feel better for adopting a positive approach to the children's behaviour.	Catch children behaving well before they have the chance to misbehave. This enables them to focus for longer.
Learning	
Ensure you have planned for the interests of the children; this will be motivating for them.	Approach lessons with enthusiasm and excitement to instil a love of the subject in the children.
Ensure you plan some tasks that you know everybody can achieve.	Differentiate your questioning for particular children to ensure achievement for all.
Recognize the strengths in all children and use these in shared teaching sessions to promote the skills and knowledge of all.	Ask specific children to complete specific parts of modelled work to demonstrate to everybody their ability to succeed.

Teaching	
Do some background research into new topics and themes so that you feel confident and competent in your teaching ability.	Prior to a new topic ask the children to do some research; everybody will have something to contribute at the start of the new theme.
If there is something you don't know, don't be afraid to tell the children that you will find out for them, or research it together.	When children say they 'can't' or they 'don't know', model the behaviour that demonstrates how to find out the information. You will enable the children to become resilient and to persevere with their learning by approaching it in this way.
Approach your teaching as a learner. If you appear to be an all-knowing being, this can create anxiety as children feel they can never match up to you.	Reward children for asking questions, for exploring ideas and for not being frightened to get things wrong. Take the blame for mistakes. 'I'm sorry I didn't explain that to you properly, let's try again.'

Research suggests that children with a good sense of self and identity, who score highly in terms of emotional intelligence tests, are less likely to fall behind at school (Whitehead 2006). These children form good relationships with their peers and school staff and demonstrate emotional resilience when situations occur in their lives that are difficult or challenging. Conversely, children with a poor sense of self, those who do not score well in emotional intelligence tests, tend to have a more turbulent time at school. They find it difficult to make friends, form relationships and persevere with tasks, showing low levels of resilience both emotionally and intellectually.

The findings of Whitehead's research showed that children who achieved high scores on emotional intelligence:

- exhibited fewer negative behaviours and emotions at school;
- were less likely to let their difficulties interfere with their peer relations and classroom learning.

These children were less likely to experience and exhibit:

- negative emotional symptoms;
- conduct problems;
- hyperactivity problems;
- problems with their peers;
- temper tantrums, lying and cheating and were generally obedient.

They were:

- less distracted;
- more able to concentrate, stay on task and think things out before acting;
- more likely to have many friends and to be liked by many children;
- less likely to pick on or bully their peers;
- rated by their teachers as being considerate of others' feelings, sharing with other children, being kind to younger children, helpful if someone is hurt, and volunteering to help others.

On the other hand, children with low levels of emotional intelligence often:

- complained of headaches;
- had many worries;
- were often unhappy, downhearted or tearful;
- were nervous or clingy in new situations;
- had many fears;
- were easily scared.

It was also noted that they seemed not to have developed effective coping strategies to help them deal with any school difficulties, classroom or peer problems that might arise.

In order to enable a good sense of self, what might we do in school to develop young people's identity, to facilitate them in developing a sense of who they are and how they cope in stressful, challenging situations?

Firstly, we need to provide children with some simple coping strategies.

THINK

Encourage children to manage their own behaviour through questioning:

- Am I angry?
- Are my words unkind or hurtful?
- Do I feel hotter than normal?
- Is my heart beating at a fast pace?
- Do I need to stop?
- Do I need some space and time alone?
- Do I need to close my eyes?
- Would I like to talk to someone about my feelings?
- Have I made someone sad?
- Do I know what I have done wrong?
- Do I know what to do to make things better?
- Do I need to apologize to someone for my behaviour?

Behaviour cannot change overnight, but by being consistent in the messages we give, by providing children with opportunities to regulate their own behaviour and understand how they feel when they are upset, we can help them to become more aware of their emotional intelligence and literacy. In time, children will be able to recognize their responses to situations and will use strategies to deal with them in an appropriate manner within the context and culture of the school.

So far, we have looked at the importance of understanding ourselves, our emotional intelligence. However, in order to develop a real sense of self, it is fundamental that we can behave in appropriate ways with others – we are social beings and our ability to function as such is dependent on our relationships with others. One could argue that in order to understand self, we have also to understand others and be aware of how our behaviour affects them. Thus it is to emotional literacy that we now turn.

Emotional literacy

Emotional literacy involves using emotions in relationships (Matthews 2006). It is about developing the self in relation to others. It is necessary to have a strong sense of who we are in order to interact with people. How we feel about ourselves is fundamental to this in terms of self-confidence, strength of character and an ability to enter into dialogue which increases and develops the self without denigrating the ideas and feelings of our peers, colleagues and pupils.

This does not only involve the way in which we speak to one another. Having the skills to read another person's body language and facial expressions is all-important; emotions reflected through these may have a direct influence on the way in which people speak and what it is they are saying. By misreading another person's emotions, we may damage the dialogue, or not fully understand the messages being signalled to us. Consequently, the relationship may be harmed or barriers may be put up as a mechanism of self-defence in order to preserve one's own ideas and thoughts.

Epstein (1998) and Greenhalgh (1994) suggest that we build our emotional understanding not so much through our experiences but in the way that we deal with them. As we live in a social culture, events and situations are constantly influencing our perception of others and ourselves. These events and situations affect us, and we in turn, through our responses, have an impact on others. It is a transactional model that is ever changing and ever evolving.

Gender and emotional development

Research that identifies differences in emotional development of boys and girls suggests that girls have superior emotional literacy to boys. Whilst it is important not to generalize, it may be useful to look at why this might be in order to redress the balance in the classroom. Evidence has shown that girls acquire greater capacity for language, and a wider vocabulary in particular, at an early age; one might argue that they acquire with this an understanding of emotional vocabulary earlier. Girls might therefore use this understanding in their play at an earlier age and be more confident in responding to and recognizing emotion than are boys.

Maines (2003) cites Hoffman (1977) as stating that girls from the age of 1 year display greater concern through more sad looks, sympathetic vocalizations and comforting than do boys. She also cites work by Connellan *et al.* (2001) that says that from birth females tend to look longer at faces, particularly at the eyes, whereas boys tend to look at inanimate objects.

Crick and Grotpeter (1995), cited by Maines (2003), suggest that boys and girls demonstrate aggression in different ways. Boys' demonstration of aggression is direct and explicit – for example, by kicking, pushing and hitting. Girls, on the other hand, use indirect methods to display their aggression through gossip, exclusion and being unkind in their words. Crick and Grotpeter propose that direct aggression requires a low level of empathy, whereas indirect aggression requires skill in reading the mind and emotional well-being of another; they suggest that its impact is strategic.

Despite this, we should not single out boys for special teaching in terms of their emotions. It is important that both boys and girls alike be provided with opportunities to develop a sense of self and how they relate to others to ensure they are able to socialize in appropriate ways in social contexts.

QUESTIONS

- How do boys and girls demonstrate their feelings within your teaching context?
- Is there a difference in the use of vocabulary during play activities or in character descriptions?
- Do either gender respond in particular ways when faced with an aggressive situation?
- How are boys and girls enabled to understand one another?
- Are there a range of role models for both genders? If not, how might this be addressed?
- How do you manage stereotyping of male and female roles?

Age and emotional development

Baron-Cohen and colleagues at the University of Cambridge (cited in Maines 2003) carried out research to explore the ages at which children understand emotions. Their research discovered, as one would probably expect, that a child's emotional vocabulary develops with age. Children aged 4–18 were asked to rate how well they understood the meaning of a word that related to an emotion. The 12–18-year-olds completed a questionnaire which allowed for one of three responses: 'clearly understood', 'not understood', and 'possibly understood'. Younger children were shown photographs of faces representing human emotion and were asked to choose words to respond to them. The research found that, by the age of 11, 75% of children understood the meaning of 114 emotion words.

Further research also supports the fact that very young children can respond to facial expressions and emotional vocalization (Mumme and Fernald, cited in Maines 2003: 9), although children below the age of 10 months tended not to be able to make the same responses. Nevertheless, the findings of Baron-Cohen reveal that 75% of children aged between 4 and 7 understand the meaning of 51 emotion words.

When children enter the Foundation Stage, much work is done to enable them to function within the new social context that they find themselves. Work is carried out to ensure they make friends, communicate effectively, respond appropriately to instructions and learn effectively in a new environment. Teachers strive to ensure that children feel secure and happy in the learning community and work hard to achieve a purposeful, positive environment for all, knowing that this will enable children to achieve well in their educational contexts.

We know from our own experiences with children that when they are frustrated, afraid or challenged, they make an emotional response. Their age and maturity will reflect the way in which they cope with these feelings. Because younger children tend to be 'taken over' by their feelings their outbursts can be disturbing: tears, soiling, aggression and withdrawal are all common patterns of behaviour in an early years setting. It does not take long for children to grow out of this behaviour as they develop greater self-awareness. Children who still display these signals as they move from class to class cause us great concern; we may discuss these children with colleagues, the SENCO or parents to find solutions for the behaviours displayed. How many of these solutions do we tie in with emotional literacy?

SCENARIO

How might this teacher work with this child to achieve a positive outcome?

I teach a class of 32 Year 4 children. There is one child in the class who is very disruptive and aggravates the children. His disruptive behaviour affects the learning and some of the less confident children appear frightened by him. He repeatedly echoes instructions I give to the class in a very loud voice, has trouble remaining in his seat for any length of time and destroys his work regularly by tearing it up or scribbling on it.

I do my best to turn a blind eye to some of the behaviour as I seem to do nothing but say his name. However, if I ignore what he is doing for long he will hurt another child. Yesterday he sharpened his pencil as sharp as it could be and then stabbed a child in the back.

Whenever I give him praise for sitting well or working nicely with the children he responds very negatively, aggressively or ignores me. I feel at the end of my tether. I keep a behaviour diary and report to his parents each day but I seem to be fighting a losing battle. What can I do?

ACTIVITY

Discuss the scenario with colleagues or peers. Many of us have experience of teaching children like this, but what can we do to help them respond to us and to their emotions?

We have considered some possible solutions; compare these with your own ideas.

- Use personal reflection to enable children to think about how their behaviour helps or hinders learning.
- Allow them time to consider how they might do things differently.
- Develop a range of tasks and activities that nurture listening skills and collaboration.
- Provide choices in the learning, giving children responsibility for and a sense of ownership of their work.
- Encourage the children to take responsibility for the behaviour of the class by offering whole-class rewards as well as individual rewards.
- Praise in a range of ways – we do not always have to praise good behaviour verbally. Try using non-verbal strategies such as a wink or a smile; give the child a note telling them how pleased you are or a sticker for their chart.
- Use emotion maps (see example below).

ACTIVITY

Take a familiar story and focus on one character who has 'ups and downs' in the narrative – Jack and the Beanstalk or Matilda, for example, or a character of your choice that links with a theme you are studying in class.

Involve the children in creating a map or a graph that charts the character's journey through the story in relation to how they feel at given points. We call this an 'emotion map'. It should include such things as sudden turns of events and unexpected reversals of fortune.

Once you have created your map/graph, consider how the character feels during the troughs and peaks of their adventure. Ask the children to think about why that character feels that way and what created those emotions. Link these to their own experiences so that the children start to recognize their own 'ups and downs' and how they worked through these to feel happy again.

Developing emotional literacy in school

School is a social community, where children are brought together in a mix of cultures from beyond the classroom, their own included. Once in the realms of the classroom these cultures may clash and children may find it difficult to understand one another. A basic principle in our day-to-day teaching should be to help each other to read and understand emotion and to be aware that facial expressions and body language link with these feelings.

ACTIVITY

Create a word bank of emotions with the children. Display these or lay them out on desks, on the carpet or on the board.

Here are the beginnings of a word bank for you:

angry	worried	excited	happy
sad	hurt	interested	surprised
sorry	sneaky	kind	bored

Practise making the facial expressions to match the emotion. You may need to model this to the children. Ask individual children to choose one of the words and to make the appropriate facial expression to represent their chosen word. Can the other children guess which word they have chosen?

Ask the children to consider how they would respond to someone who looks like this. How will they approach someone who is feeling that particular emotion? Do they need to change the way they would usually approach that person to be considerate to their feelings?

Following on from this, ask the children to sort the words into categories that represent whether these emotions have a positive or negative effect on themselves and others.

Can the children remember a time when they felt a particular emotion? How did they react? How did others react towards them? Did their behaviour affect others? Did others affect the way they felt? How might they respond differently another time if the feelings created a negative response?

Take photographs of the children as they make the different facial expressions and display them with the word bank.

Create a book together that provides suggestions and strategies for making people feel better, or that suggest ways to respond to people when they are feeling a particular way.

Approaches for developing emotional intelligence and literacy in school: R time

The R time approach is an exciting and dynamic development in personal and social education. It was developed in 2002 and is a whole-school approach that has a positive impact on social inclusion, contentment in school, relationships and promoting a positive school ethos (Osborn 2006). The R time approach is designed to fit with the Social and Emotional Aspects of Learning (SEAL) materials from the Primary National Strategy.

The approach focuses on how children relate to one another and how to enable all to relate well. This approach is a positive way to maintain and develop the excellent work already practised in schools to improve and accelerate learning and self-esteem. The fundamental nature of R time is the combination of five component parts within weekly lessons lasting between 15 and 20 minutes (http://www.rtime.info/approach.htm):

- *Random pairing*. This is where the children work with a different partner each time enabling them to develop relationships with all the others in the class.
- *Introductions*. This involves greeting one another with a positive statement: 'Hello, my name is Katie. I am glad I am working with you today, Simon.'
- *The activity*. These are age appropriate activities for the different year groups for partner work. Talking about a hobby, an interest, how you are feeling and so on.
- *Plenary*. This provides children with the opportunity to give feedback to the class, with the teacher facilitating, in order to reflect on the activity.
- *Conclusion*. The children thank their partner and finish their session with a positive statement.

Social and Emotional Aspects of Learning

The SEAL resource (DCSF 2007) provides a framework for explicitly promoting social, emotional and behavioural skills, with built-in progression for each year group within a school. The resource is designed to facilitate a systematic and spiral approach to learning. It should be seen as a stimulus or starting point, rather than a finished product. It is hoped that it will provide structured support to the creativity and initiative of schools who use the materials.

The materials include a guidance booklet, a 'Getting started' poster, and a whole-school resource with photocards. There are seven sets of thematic materials that each have:

- an assembly and overview;
- a Red set booklet – for the Foundation Stage;
- a Blue set booklet – for Years 1 and 2;
- a Yellow set booklet – for Years 3 and 4;
- a Green set booklet – for Years 5 and 6.

The SEAL resource is designed to support schools in the work they are doing to develop the school as a community that promotes social, emotional and behavioural skills. The resource provides several elements that are designed to be used across the whole school community. These include: guidance and continuing professional development; assemblies; and work with parents and carers.

TeacherNet (2007) describes SEAL for primary schools as follows:

> Primary SEAL offers a whole-school framework for promoting the social and emotional aspects of learning: self-awareness, managing feelings, motivation, empathy and social skills. Primary SEAL is organized into seven themes which can be covered within a school year:
>
> - New Beginnings
> - Getting on and falling out
> - Say no to Bullying
> - Going for goals!
> - Good to be me
> - Relationships
> - Changes

A healthy sense of self-esteem forms the corner-stone of constructive relationships with others. Those children who feel good about themselves and see themselves in a positive light are more likely to feel positive about those around them. It has been suggested that children who appreciate their own intrinsic value are less likely to tolerate discrimination and inequality. As teachers, we are aware of the correlation between academic achievement and social and emotional development.

> The Primary SEAL resource is intended to build on the effective work that many schools and settings are already doing to develop social and emotional skills, and can be used flexibly. Some schools for example may choose to address social and emotional skills through core and Foundation subjects.
>
> (TeacherNet 2007)

This curriculum resource aims to develop the underpinning qualities and skills that help promote positive behaviour and effective learning. It focuses on five social and emotional aspects of learning: self-awareness, managing feelings, motivation, empathy and social skills.

The materials help children develop skills such as understanding another's point of view, working in a group, sticking at things when they get difficult, resolving conflict and managing worries. They build on effective work already in place in the many primary schools who pay systematic attention to the social and emotional aspects of learning through whole-school ethos, initiatives such as circle time or buddy schemes, and the taught PSHE and citizenship curriculum.

Special educational needs

All children will challenge rules and authority at times often just to test the boundaries, but although they break them, children need rules to make them feel secure. Some children are particularly challenging, and need clear guidelines to help them in their development of their own behaviour management. Understanding how they feel when they get angry, upset or frustrated is an important step in regulating challenging behaviour. For our children with special needs in relation to their behaviour we need to put in place additional guidelines to ensure that they remain safe and that others are not harmed as a result of an outburst. Building on the content of Chapter 3, we can help to manage these behaviours by:

- If a child is in a potentially disturbing situation, try to remove him/her from it.
  E.g. If he/she is being confronted by another child in the class, divert his/her attention by asking him/her to fetch someone for you.
  Make sure all staff that are likely to be in contact with the pupil are aware of the problem and have an agreed strategy to deal with situations.
- Try to explain [the] problem to peers and ask for their help in alerting you to potential problem situations.
- Introduce new work concepts very slowly and cautiously and give rewards regularly for success.
- Try to discover the interests of the child and build a sense of friendship through them.
- If the child does have a temper tantrum, do not confront him. If he/she is in danger of hurting himself/herself or others, he/she may need [to be] restrained. Try to put [him/her] somewhere he/she can be on his/her own.
- Encourage a pupil to indicate when he/she is feeling particularly upset. This could be done by drawing unhappy faces at particular stages of his/her work or in a daily record chart etc. Analysis of this might enable the detection of particular trigger factors.

(http://scotens.org/sen/teaching/emotionalstrat.html)

Top Tips

TOP TIPS		
Pre-empt behaviour. As the children come to sit down, praise the child who normally fidgets before they have a chance to fidget. They will sit still for that little bit longer.	Try to understand the reason for the behaviour. Remember you do not have to do this with words. Perhaps the child would prefer to make a drawing.	Where possible, use non-verbal strategies. Simply remove the object the child is fiddling with rather than asking them to put it down. This prevents disrupting the flow of your teaching.

Make instructions simple: stop, look, wait, etc.	Be clear in your language: I want you to ..., I need you to .... Keep choice to a minimum.	Once an incident has been dealt with, move on from it. Try not to let the behaviour upset the rest of the class or the rest of the day.

Co-operative learning strategies allow children and young people to experience their social connections not as separate individuals but as an interrelated system in which the actions of each member affect, and are affected by, the actions of others. The ability to listen and ask questions and the opportunity to express oneself are fundamental in the emotional development of children in our schools. The various aspects of emotional literacy are listed by Katherine Weare (2004: 3–4) as follows:

Self-understanding
- Having an accurate and positive view of ourselves.
- Having a sense of optimism about the world and ourselves.
- Having a coherent and continuous life story.

Understanding and managing emotions
- Experiencing the whole range of emotions.
- Understanding the causes of our emotions.
- Expressing our emotions appropriately.
- Managing our responses to our emotions effectively, for example managing our anger, controlling our impulses.
- Knowing how to feel good more often and for longer.
- Using information about emotions to plan and solve problems.
- Resilience – processing, and bouncing back from, difficult experiences.

Understanding social situations and making relationships
- Forming attachments to other people.
- Experiencing empathy for others.
- Communicating and responding effectively to others.
- Managing our relationships effectively.
- Being autonomous: independent and self-reliant.

In order to do this successfully we need to ensure that children are secure in their sense of self. Self-esteem develops as a result of interpersonal relationships; it develops throughout childhood and adolescence and into later life. For the school-age child parents, teachers and peers fundamentally affect self-esteem. It can be regarded as how we rate our self-image – certain characteristics or abilities have a greater value in society and this has an inherent influence on the development of self-esteem, self-knowledge and self-awareness.

Top Tips

TOP TIP

Put a box in the classroom where children can post messages anonymously about how they are feeling. Monitor it regularly, and use the messages as starting points for class discussion.

CONSIDERATION

Read the following note that a Year 5 child has posted.

> Sometimes I feel worried about sharing my ideas or putting my hand up in case my answer is wrong. I want to be part of discussions but I don't feel confident enough to share what I think in group situations.

How will you approach this with your class?

What questions might you ask the children to help this child?

What might you need to do to change your practice to ensure that everybody can contribute his or her ideas in a safe environment?

What different ways are there for children to make a suggestion or share an idea?

By providing opportunities in school for children to recognize and regulate negative aspects of behaviour, we are helping them to interact and adapt to social contexts not only in school but also in their local community. This emotional understanding cannot be underestimated if we are to ensure that young people lead safe and healthy lives, make the right choices and have healthy relationships. Chapter 6 provides creative strategies for raising children's self-esteem.

KEY POINTS

- Emotional intelligence and emotional literacy are two different entities.
- To be effective teachers we need to care for our own emotional well-being as well as the emotional stability of our young people.
- Helping children to recognize how they respond to their emotions can enable them to develop a sense of self.
- By providing children with opportunities to recognize how others sometimes feel, we can help them to consider how to approach different situations.

5   Policy into practice

In this chapter, we will look at how an effective whole-school policy for behaviour management can help you to develop a consistent, coherent approach to managing behaviour in the primary school. We will focus on:

- the importance of a whole-school policy to behaviour management;
- the way in which policies are formulated;
- how a policy can be seen in practice;
- long-term policy benefits;
- the way in which a policy operates in the medium term, classroom management and organization, rules, routines and relationships;
- quick-fire strategies for managing behaviour in the short term, including gaining attention, working together, self-presentation and affirming statements.

A whole-school policy

Schools should have a clear vision for managing behaviour through establishing clear rules and boundaries, with emphasis on the positive. In formulating a policy in the primary school, it is most important to ensure that there is an agreed message, philosophy and understanding of which everybody is aware, in order to achieve a consistent and coherent approach throughout the school. If we use one method of behaviour management and a colleague uses a different method altogether, this can lead to confusion, uncertainty and inconsistency for both pupils and staff alike. Having a behaviour management policy in place means that there is clear direction for all involved, and that includes the adults as well as the children.

Consistency is key, and for this to be effective, it is crucial that we adopt a holistic approach to formulating the policy, whereby teaching staff, non-teaching staff, pupils, governors and local community members are consulted and their ideas applied to the policy.

A policy should reflect the ethos of the school and the way in which it wishes to enable the young people who attend it to engage in all aspects of their education from day to day. An effective policy should act as a safeguard for both pupils and staff and should communicate to school, local and wider communities the expectations of all those who work within it. In Chapter 1 we explore the idea of school ethos and mission statements.

Legislation on behaviour policies and related areas came into force in England and Wales on 1 April 2007. This legislation appears in sections 88–96 of the Education and Inspections Act 2006 (this can be accessed by visiting http://www.opsi.gov.uk/acts/acts2006a.htm). The new law follows a report by the practitioners' group on school behaviour and discipline. Because of this report, the government set out its commitments for improving school discipline – in the White Paper, *Higher Standards, Better Education for All* (Education and Skills Committee 2006).

The 2006 Act carries forward those commitments, including the establishment of a statutory power to enforce school discipline, and more specific measures relating to excluded pupils and to parental responsibility for the behaviour of children.

The guidance is meant to be the centrepiece of a suite of new and updated guidance on behaviour-related issues. It is intended to be a source of reference for schools on legal powers and duties, with a focus on explaining what these mean in practical terms.

The guidance on developing and implementing a behaviour policy for head teachers and other school staff is non-statutory, although schools are advised to follow the guidance. There are, however, statutory responsibilities for the governing body of a school. The governing body is responsible for putting together the underlying principles of the policy that will guide the head teacher in the process. The Education and Inspections Act 2006 also requires governors to consult on the principles contained within the policy, which includes the pupil voice.

ACTIVITY

Using a copy of your current behaviour management policy, consider how it reflects the ethos of your school. Underline sections where you see this policy in practice, and consider where you see it and how. Also, underline sections that are not seen in practice: why might this be?

Now think about some of the practice you have observed or experienced that is not reflected in the policy. Is this because the practice is poor or because some staff members have specific ways of dealing with behaviour?

How can these be incorporated into the policy? Is there a need for staff development, where staff members who are particularly effective in their behaviour management could share good practice? How might the policy be updated, reviewed or rewritten?

In writing a policy, the culture and 'personality' of the school should be carefully considered. It is important to be aware of what these are. What is the personality of your school? This will be made up of the relationships between staff, children and the community within and beyond the school. It is unique and exclusive to your school, and should be celebrated for being so. Porter (2007) states that a policy will be useless, perhaps even obstructive, when it is inconsistent with the culture of a school. We might be tempted to adapt a policy from another school and to use that in our daily routines. It is wise not to do this, as this policy will have been created to fit in with the ethos, personality and culture of that specific school. Your own school will need to seek ways to ensure its own voice is heard. We will discuss this in more detail later.

The long-term view

For successful behaviour management in all aspects of school life it is essential that we do not view policy and practice as two separate entities. They are inextricably linked, and practice should be at the heart of the policy for it to be truly triumphant. Before we look at how to create a policy it might first be useful to consider the salient features of your school. What is the culture of your school?

REFLECT

Take a moment to think about the school in which you are based.

• What is the initial feeling you get as soon as you enter the school?
• How warm and welcoming is the entrance?
• Are there signs to greet you, or messages about expectations in the school?
• Is the mission statement displayed?
• Is the atmosphere a positive one?
• Who are the different people who help to make up the personality of your school?

Now think about the relationships of the staff and pupils.

• Do the staff get along?
• Is there laughter in the workplace?
• Are the values and expectations of pupils reflected in the way staff conduct their relationships with one another?
• Do all staff use positive language? Is their energy good?
• How do staff relate to pupils?
• Is it evident that pupils are liked?
• Are the children valued and respected? Is this evident in the language staff use?

Now think about the children.

- Is it evident that the children are happy?
- Is the work that is on display a celebration of the children's efforts?
- Do the children speak to one another in a caring way?
- Is it evident that they have good relationships with the teachers and support staff?
- Is it evident that the children have good relationships with one another?
- Is the noise in school a happy buzz of productive chatter and discussion?

Note some of your thoughts and responses. What sort of place is your school? What is the culture there? How has the personality of your school been formed?

Writing a policy

We mentioned earlier that for the policy to be effective it was essential that all stakeholders should have an input and a voice. We would recommend that you follow a plan of action; we have provided a suggested outline for this below. But before you start to write your policy, discuss collectively what you expect the outcomes to be. What do you want from the policy? Discuss what you mean by good behaviour. Create a definition of this that will be at the heart of your policy – after all, that is what you will all be striving to achieve.

ACTIVITY

Write down your definition of good behaviour.

When we think about behaviour we often relate it to the way in which we engage with one another. Behaviour is of course related to this, but let us not forget that it encompasses a great deal more besides. An important part of the policy should be to consider all aspects of behaviour, not solely relationships. This may include:

- the school environment;
- classrooms;
- relationships;
- playtime;
- lunchtime behaviour;
- after-school clubs;
- behaviour out of school (trips);
- behaviour in the community.

Of course this list is not exhaustive, and you may think of more to add to it.

Responsibility

Responsibility lies firstly with the governors. The responsibilities of the governing body for discipline as stated by section 88 of the Education and Inspections Act 2006 are as follows:

(1) The governing body of a relevant school must ensure that policies designed to promote good behaviour and discipline on the part of its pupils are pursued at the school.

(2) In particular, the governing body –
    (a) must make, and from time to time review, a written statement of general principles to which the head teacher is to have regard in determining any measures under section 89(1), and
    (b) where they consider it desirable that any particular measures should be so determined by the head teacher or that he should have regard for any particular matters –
        (i) shall notify him of those measures or matters, and
        (ii) may give him such guidance as they consider appropriate.

Process

Consider first what you hope to achieve from the policy; meet with staff, children, parents and community members to establish this. Try to approach the policy writing process from a positive standpoint whereby you think about what your expectations are, in terms of what the children do well and on how this can be built upon. Describe the sort of behaviour you want to promote. This may come from your discussions about what you believe good behaviour to be and what you want for the children you teach.

The process of formulating the policy should consist of the following steps:

1. *Consultation.* Ensure you consult all stakeholders; it is essential that every viewpoint is considered in the process.
2. *Draft.* Once you have collated each response, you can begin to create a draft policy.
3. *Consensus.* Once the draft is complete, consult again with the different stakeholders to ensure they are all in agreement with the policy and that they are aware of its contents.
4. *Review.* At this point, you can amend and adapt what has been written to ensure that the contents are fit for purpose.
5. *Implementation.* Implement the policy; guide both staff and pupils in the process of implementation to ensure success. Agree a date for the feedback once the policy has had time to establish.
6. *Feedback.* Use the feedback to develop the policy further. Progress can be measured to determine the effectiveness of the policy in order to evaluate the impact on behaviour. This will bring you back to the consultation stage. What worked? What needs changing? Set a date for consultation to develop the policy further.

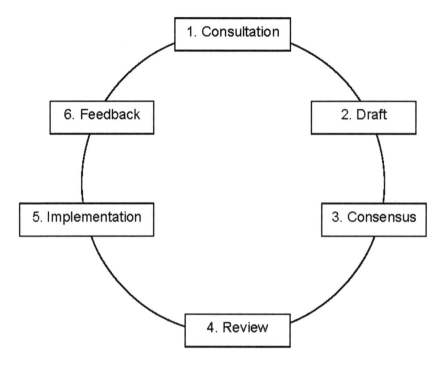

Figure 1 Policy formulation process

This process should be cyclical (see Figure 1) in order to ensure that the policy is reviewed, adapted and monitored regularly. If things are not working, you can change them, but what is essential is that the policy is not allowed to become stagnant. It should be evolving and growing as you become better acquainted with how well it has been implemented and how well it is working.

The systems and strategies that have been included in the policy should be embedded into the daily life of the school. Draw attention to the rules and apply them regularly and consistently. The policy should be accessible to all those who will engage in the life of the school. That way your message will be clear and there will be no inconsistencies in its application.

Rules within the policy should be short, clear and realistic. It may be necessary and advisable to differentiate these in order that they are age appropriate for the children. Provide access for parents to view the policy so that they too can apply the consistent messages you wish to embrace. It may be that you produce a home–school agreement that has these messages clearly stated within it. Ensure you are well informed about the policy so that you apply it fairly and appropriately.

Do take account of the different cultures, backgrounds and upbringings of the children in the school when you implement and apply strategies. We must not forget that what is acceptable and right in one culture may not apply in another. For example, you may wish children to look at you when you are talking to them about their behaviour. In some cultures, this is deemed to be disrespectful, so think carefully about how the policy can be practically applied to meet the needs of all concerned.

What happens when the behaviour you are working to achieve does not materialize? This is an important part of your review and feedback. The rewards are significant and so are the sanctions. Have you got this right? Apply a staged approach; Chapter 6 looks at this in more detail, and we will discuss systems and strategies later in this chapter, but in summary:

- On the first occasion we will ...
- If the behaviour is repeated the same day we will ...
- If the behaviour continues we will ...

(Teaching Expertise 2006)

Of course, we should maintain the positive perspective and consider what we will do when we do see the behaviour we are striving to achieve. This should come in the form of reward; both extrinsic and intrinsic rewards are essential. By reinforcing and consolidating good behaviour, we will continue to help children to rise to the expectations we set and the behaviour that they too desire.

For implementation in the long term, we need to consider the long-term planning of the curriculum to ensure that messages pervade into teaching and learning. This should take into consideration equal opportunities within the classroom, extracurricular activities and behaviour strategies. All strategies should be applied equally to both boys and girls, regardless of age, gender, race, nationality or ability. This has implications for the way in which behaviour is sanctioned and rewarded, as it must consider cultural and emotional differences for it to be truly effective.

Within curriculum planning, we should identify specific areas that will allow teaching and learning of social skills, emotional understanding and development of self and identity. These aspects are considered in some detail in Chapter 4. It would be sensible to assume that PSHE, citizenship and SEAL may embed the principles and practices of the school ethos and policy in relation to positive behaviour. Schools may also use RE to engage in such learning as well as collective worship time. In planning the long-term curriculum areas we would suggest using stories and pictures to engage pupils in the social development of themselves as well as in developing empathy towards the feelings, beliefs and attitudes of others. Stories can be a powerful motivator for learning about the self from a distance whilst still enabling children to make links to their own situations and experiences. This is explored in Chapter 7, and there are some suggested activities for such learning in the classroom environment.

CONSIDERATION

Take an area of the curriculum and consider how you might embed the behaviour policy within it. Consider this together with a colleague for the different age groups you teach or have taught on a placement. Think about:

- the language of the policy to match the needs and ages of pupils;
- progression from year group to year group and key stage to key stage;
- appropriate rewards and sanctions that follow a consistent process;
- stories and themes that might be a starting point for the medium-term planning.

Supporting one another in the long term is essential to avoid burnout. Porter (2007) discusses the way in which collegial support can aid as a buffer against stress in teachers. She argues that organizational stress can be a better predictor of burnout in teachers than actual teaching challenges. This is something that can be built into the policy at the point of writing.

Being open about the challenges we face in terms of our behaviour management means that we do not feel alone when children are behaving inappropriately. Sharing good practice and offering solutions to problems can help to solve some of the difficulties we face. Assigning ownership to ensure success, if our decisions and ideas are listened to and incorporated into teaching and learning situations, we are more likely to consider the impact of what we are doing collectively. Consequently, we will strive to make it successful.

If we as teachers demonstrate good relationships by the way we interact with each other, the children are more likely to mirror this behaviour in their relationships. We should also recognize and celebrate our achievements and share these with the pupils when we crack a particularly difficult problem. All of these elements need to be considered in the long-term decisions we make as a school.

Policy in the medium term

This section looks at the medium-term elements of the policy. These elements relate to the way in which the systems in the classroom allow the policy to live and grow on a daily basis. We will consider a range of elements that are involved such as expectations, rules and relationships.

SCENARIO

David is a newly qualified teacher. He has just started his first post in an inner-city primary school. There are two weeks to go before the start of term and David has gone into school to set up his classroom. What does he need to consider in order to make the first day and hopefully the rest of the week and term successful?

QUESTIONS

- Discuss the different elements of his classroom organization with a colleague or peer and think about the way in which these decisions will impact on and influence behaviour in the classroom.

- List the things he needs to take into consideration.
- How do these elements relate to the behaviour of the children both negatively and positively?
- What can he do before the children arrive for their first day at school?
- What should he do on the first day with the children?
- What elements of the organization and management of the class can be done together with the children?
- Why is this important?
- What advice would you offer David on his first day?

If you are a newly qualified or trainee teacher, you have yet to establish your personality within the school environment. Many trainee teachers at the beginning of their training are of the impression that being friends with the children is important. We learn all too quickly that this is not the case. Caring for, listening to and nurturing those children is of course important, but it is not our role to be their friend in the same way they themselves form friendships. Therefore, at the start of the year, whether you are newly qualified or an experienced teacher, the way in which you elucidate your expectations will be all-important in how you engage with your class.

The Elton (1989) report, although commissioned by the government in 1989, remains a seminal document today. It establishes connections with the curriculum and overall classroom management and organization. Further to this, everybody involved in the planning, delivery and evaluation of the curriculum should recognize that the quality of teaching and learning has a significant impact on children's behaviour (TeacherNet n.d.).

Elton (1989: 68) provides the following guidance in terms of good practice; it is drawn from a range of teachers, observations and materials:

teachers should:

27.1 know pupils as individuals. This means knowing their names, their personalities and interests and who their friends are;

27.2 plan and organise both the classroom and the lesson to keep pupils interested and minimise the opportunities for disruption. This requires attention to such basics as furniture layout, grouping of pupils, matching work to pupils' abilities, pacing lessons well, being enthusiastic and using humour to create a positive classroom atmosphere;

27.3 be flexible in order to take advantage of unexpected events rather than being thrown off balance by them. Examples would include the appearance of the window cleaner or a wasp in the middle of a lesson;

27.4 continually observe or 'scan' the behaviour of a class;

27.5 be aware of, and control their own behaviour, including stance and tone of voice;

27.6 model the standards of courtesy they expect from their pupils;

27.7 emphasise the positive, including praise for good behaviour as well as good work;

27.8   make the rules for classroom behaviour clear to pupils from the first lesson and explain why they are necessary;

27.9   make sparing and consistent use of reprimands. This means being firm rather than aggressive, targeting the right pupil, criticising the behaviour and not the person, using private rather than public reprimands whenever possible, being fair and consistent, and avoiding sarcasm and idle threats;

27.10   make sparing and consistent use of punishments. This includes avoiding whole group punishment which pupils see as unfair. It also means avoiding punishments which humiliate pupils by, for example, making them look ridiculous. This breeds resentment; and

27.11   analyse their own classroom management performance and learn from it. This is the most important message of all.

Let us take these messages provided by the report and consider how they can be used to help David in his NQT year. How many of the points stated were linked to or were included in the advice you came up with?

> ACTIVITY
>
> Group the different statements in relation to the classroom.
>
> | Children's behaviour | Teachers' behaviour |
> | --- | --- |
> | | |
> | Environment and curriculum | Reflection and analysis |
> | | |
>
> - 'Learning well' means that children need a calm and purposeful classroom atmosphere.
> - Children need their teacher to be able to take control and to deal with behavioural issues in a clam and consistent way in order that they feel safe and secure in the learning environment.
> - Reflecting on and analysing our own behaviour is important, but only if we learn from our mistakes and change our practice to best suit the needs of our pupils.

Establishing the expectations

On the first day back at school following the long summer break, children experience a range of emotions from excitement and joy, to anxiety and resentment. It is fundamental in the first few minutes to establish expectations together. This will manifest itself firstly in the way in which the children are greeted, settled and welcomed into your classroom. Getting this right will dictate feelings, emotions and behaviour for the rest of the school year. What do you expect from the children, what do they expect from you, and what do they expect from one another?

Establish the rules for your classroom together; assign responsibility and ownership to the children. Talk about 'our classroom' as opposed to 'my classroom' or 'your classroom'. Display the rules where they can be seen and take some time to ensure that everybody is clear about what the expectations are. Ensure you have linked these systems to the policy that has been established, so that there is a coherent message throughout the school. Be sure to model the behaviour you expect from the children in all aspects of the teaching day. The children will look to you to do this.

TOP TIPS

- Think before you act.
- Maintain high expectations.
- Be positive.
- Consistency and clarity are key.
- Remember that you are the adult – do not enter into disagreements.
- Have a small number of rules and consolidate them through praise.
- Keep rules simple and clear.
- Practise rules and routines regularly.

The learning environment

The learning environment can have an influence on the way in which children behave. In Chapter 7 we explore some of these ideas, but for now let us think about what an effective learning environment looks and feels like. Classrooms that are tidy and organized create feelings of calm and purpose for both the children and the adults working within them.

CONSIDER

- What are the different areas of your classroom?
- What do they look like?
- How is the children's work valued in the classroom?
- What does the room look like to an outsider?

- Do you enjoy working in your classroom?
- Are resources easily accessible?
- Are there clear signs and labels around the room?
- Does the classroom layout help or hinder learning?

Some areas you might have considered are the following:

Cloakroom	Sink/wet area	Your desk
Children's desks	Display boards	Bookshelves
Reading corner	Role-play area	Drawer units and resources
Display tables	Carpet area	Windows

First of all, consider how inviting these areas are for the children and the way in which you organize these areas. We have taken three of the areas and provided some strategies and ideas for keeping them tidy.

The cloakroom

Are coats hung or flung? We had a lovely coat rack in our school, but it was too high for the children for whom it was intended and as a result coats and bags were difficult to hang. Make sure that all coat racks and pegs are at an appropriate height for the children using them. Provide the children with responsibility for the cloakroom area. All pegs should be labelled clearly and all coats and bags should be hung neatly. It may be necessary to practise this routine at the start of the year. Keep a box in the area for lost property and fallen objects. Employ 'cloakroom attendants' who can keep an eye on the neatness and tidiness of the area.

Drawer units and resources

We tend to keep resources in these, but is it clear what and where those things are within the units? Label drawers with a word and a picture so that children can easily access the resources they need on a regular basis. Count the scissors; stick a label inside the drawer stating the number so that they can be counted out and counted back in.

Collect small boxes to go inside drawers for storing small objects neatly. Provide a few minutes in the timetable for tidying up properly so you are not pressurized to do it all at the end of the day. If boxes are kept on top of units, label them clearly on all sides; stick a small label on the wall to give the box a place to live. Ask the children to make labels and to decide where things should go; they are more likely to keep things tidy if they have ownership and responsibility.

If resources are shabby, throw them out. It is better to have a small range of high-quality resources than large numbers of resources that are not used by the children. If there are particular resources that are used regularly by the children keep them in boxes without lids to save time in lessons. Any resources that are used infrequently can be stored on shelves out of the way, or in a central place for all school staff to share.

Keep the resources in the same place and always put them back there. This way you establish a routine for both yourself and the children. Respect the different objects and storage containers by cleaning them out and washing them when they get grubby.

The reading corner

Use your reading corner to promote a theme or topic that the children are studying in class. Display the books you wish children to refer to within easy reach to avoid disruption. Have several copies of popular magazines or articles for reference. This will provide the chance for discussion of the same topic and prevent a 'queue' for a book, or an argument when someone else is reading the book.

Provide questions, quizzes and puzzles relating to topics so that the children can engage at different levels and have a focus for an activity. This will cut down chatter and silly behaviour in the area.

Consider where the area is placed within the classroom – can you see all the children? How many children can go into the area at a given time? Is there somewhere to sit? Is the area clean and tidy? Are there storage systems in place for books not being used or for the organization of the space? Use different coloured boxes for different reading items; colour code the reading material to enable the children to put it back where it belongs when they have finished. Place notices in and around the area to remind the children how to behave. For example:

- 'This is a quiet place, please respect other readers in this area.'
- 'Discuss books together, politely, quietly and with respect for each other's viewpoints.'
- 'Please put things back from where you got them.'
- 'Thank you for remembering to work quietly in here.'

The classroom should feel busy and vibrant, it should be a place of excitement and interest, where learning is valued, loved and nurtured. Instil your love of learning in the children by working together to make the environment one that you can all share happily.

Rules

Although we are guided by the behaviour policy in terms of rewards, sanctions and approaches to behaviour in the classroom, each of us will no doubt have certain expectations and routines that apply to our individual situations and the children and young people we teach. Set about making rules as a joint effort. Work together to develop a rule pattern that everyone understands and agrees with. This will provide a coherent, consistent approach, ensures everyone has a voice and helps all involved to adhere to the systems put in place.

TOP TIPS

- Keep rules simple and write them in child-friendly language.

- Reinforce and consolidate rules regularly.

- Make them short and snappy. They will be easier to remember.

- Learn rules and routines with music and actions.

- Display them where they can be easily seen and read by the children.

- Explain the rules to avoid ambiguity and misunderstandings.

Relationships

The relationships we build with the children we teach are varied and diverse. Although it is essential to be consistent, the very nature of personalities means that our relationships in the classroom will alter with the different children we teach. Some children are very easy to get along with: they are happy to be in school, they like you and they get along with everybody in the class. Others are more difficult: they may not like coming to school, they may not like you and they may find it difficult to make friendships. Children's emotional development will have evolved at different rates; this was discussed in detail in the previous chapter. Regardless of any of these factors, it is our professional duty to form strong and healthy relationships with our pupils. We will all have come across the child who knows it all, or the child who tells lies, or the child who wants our undivided attention. These children can take up much of our time and energy, but there are reasons underlying these behaviours and we must rise above traits that can be exasperating and find the good that lies within.

CONSIDERATION

Choose two children you teach or have taught: one child who is/was easy going and friendly, and another who is/was more difficult to manage, call them A and B respectively. In the table below, consider the personality traits of and behaviours displayed by each child.

Child A	Child B

> Now consider the different ways in which you respond to each child in relation to that behaviour and those traits. What are the similarities and differences and why?

We can feel irritated and frustrated by certain behaviours. This is normal and, so long as we identify these feelings within ourselves, we can work on levelling out our responses to ensure our relationships are equal within the classroom. If we did a time tally, we might well discover that more of our attention is given to those who behave more inappropriately than those who just simply get on with the day-to-day routines in the classroom. What might you do to provide more equal opportunities for each child you teach?

We suggest some of the following to build effective relationships:

- Be interested in what everybody has to say.
- Ask questions.
- Let the children know you are interested in their hobbies and interests by providing opportunities for everybody to share.
- Use praise to encourage the behaviour you expect.

Policy in the short term

So far we have considered writing the policy, implementing the policy and working together in the classroom to promote and encourage good behaviour. On a day-to-day basis we need a range of strategies up our sleeves to help us through stressful moments, different lessons and a range of situations. We acquire these as we gain more experience and can learn from other professionals with whom we work. Try to anticipate good behaviour to prevent poor behaviour. Know your boundaries and be clear about what you expect. Be aware of how you are feeling too and use positive strategies to avoid losing control. This section provides a range of different ways for dealing with behaviour in the short term.

What sort of teacher are you?

Aspects of this were considered in Chapter 1. Let us now further explore ourselves as teachers. Are you aware of what you think about the children in the class? Are there aspects of your behaviour management that you would like to improve or work on? Have you considered how you present yourself? Your tone of voice, your stance, your body language and your presentation will all have a direct impact on how you are perceived by the children and, in turn, on how they respond to you.

Voice

Your voice is all-important. The way you speak can motivate, excite, enthuse and manage the children; conversely, it can frighten, bore, disappoint and dampen their spirits. We are not all blessed with the rich voice of an actor, but then neither were they necessarily; they were taught how to use it effectively. Tone of voice and intonation are essential aspects for promoting the positive responses we want from our pupils, and this takes time and training. Our breathing supports our voice. When we are stressed our breathing quickens and our body tenses, and this has a direct impact on the voice. So at all times try to remain calm and remember to breathe slowly and calmly. Try warming up your voice before you start the day and practise articulation to be clear and eloquent in your speech. Some vocal warm-ups could include the following:

- A deep low hum, followed, once established, by raising the pitch, and raising it again. Reverse the exercise.
- Horse buzzes and drilling the tongue.

Here are some tongue twisters to help you articulate:

- The bloke's back brake block broke.
- She stood upon the balcony inexplicably hiccupping and amicably welcoming him in.
- Hot proper coffee in a copper coffee pot.

Stance

The way we stand affects our voice, so whenever possible try to stand straight so that your diaphragm best supports your voice. Think also about the message your stance gives to your class. If we stand straight and tall when we are doing direct teaching, we look ready for action, can move about easily and feel professional and in control. A sloppy stance gives the message that we are bored, disinterested or lazy. If you slouch, so will the children. There is a fine balance between having a good stance and looking like you are on patrol – you do not want to frighten the children, so get the balance right. Move about the room as you teach, to maintain interest and to keep your class attentive.

Body language

This too creates messages. Be open; try not to fold your arms, as this gives the impression you are creating a barrier. Use your hands, but try not to point at children too much as this can appear aggressive. Think about what your body says about how interested you are in the children.

Presentation

We are not all lucky enough to have fantastic wardrobes, but being presentable is important. It shows that you care about yourself. If you look like you care about yourself, you create the impression that you will probably also care about others. We know that for different reasons some children come to school in dirty clothes, or that they have poor hygiene, and we are sensitive to this. We also know that these children are not always terribly popular with their peers. Think about what your presentation says about you. Presentation links also to the professional persona we demonstrate and this links to the voice, the way we stand and the way we use our body.

Motivation

We can help children to achieve their potential by motivating them. Motivational strategies can be extrinsic and intrinsic. Use non-verbal as well as verbal praise. A thumbs up, a wink, a nod or a smile tells a child at a glance that you are pleased with their behaviour. Non-verbal strategies also mean that you do not always have to disrupt the teaching and learning that is taking place.

Stickers, team points and special stamps motivate children, and they will try harder to please and to repeat the behaviour you have rewarded. Special privileges can have the same effect, for example: standing at the front of line, sitting in the magic chair, being the class champion for the day. Displaying behaviour awards is important too; so that we can all recognize times when we have done well. Ensure that everybody has an award, even if it is for the smallest thing; we all need to feel good about ourselves.

Behaviour targets

Targets may be set to focus on specific behaviours we are trying to achieve. Whole-class targets can create a sense of collegiality as we all strive to reach the same goal. Try not to remove rewards from whole-class targets, as this could cause resentment, especially in those who always behave well. Whether these are group or individual targets, they should be achievable, short and simple so that they can be remembered. Giving targets a short life means that the child can be rewarded quickly for improvement rather than finally getting that long-desired certificate on the last day of term.

Sanctions

Sanctions should be used carefully and in line with the policy. Do not remove rewards for good behaviour given earlier in the day. This destroys the child's self-confidence and takes away the achievement they celebrated at that point in time. Do not use a sanction that affects the whole class because of one child's behaviour. PE should never be used as a sanction; we would not say 'If you do that again you are not doing mathematics'. Remember that staying in at playtime is not always a sanction for those children who do not want to go outside. If you feel you cannot cope with a child, calmly send them to another teacher with a behaviour buddy and a note explaining what the child has done to upset the classroom atmosphere. Be careful what you write – they might read it so keep it professional. Do not ignore inappropriate behaviour. To ignore it is to condone it. Also strike a balance: sometimes it is better to make it known that you have seen the undesirable actions – your eyes and your facial expression may be enough to act as a caution. Be consistent, follow your rules and use a warning system before you impose the sanction. Always allow the opportunity for the child to reflect on their behaviour and to put right what they have done wrong; that way you get the balance back.

Celebrate achievement

We talked earlier about motivation: good behaviour should be celebrated at all times. When children behave well, tell them and let others know how pleased you are with their behaviour. Others will rise to meet the expectations you have set together. Thank children for doing the right thing and making the right choice. Tell their parents or send a note home so their achievement can be celebrated there too. Have systems in place for celebration: three cheers, a sound effect of a round of applause, or a special song that the children have chosen for that purpose. We met a teacher recently who gives out 'Smithies', which are his version of the Oscars.

Gaining attention

Use different ways to gain the attention of the children. Some of these may already be part of the established routines, but an element of the unexpected can have surprising results.

- Use a musical instrument – the harmonica is a favourite of ours.
- Clap a pattern that has a predictable response.
- Chant a phrase that has a reply: 'Are we ready?' 'Yes we are!'
- Follow my leader – make a pattern with your hand in the air to be followed by the class.
- Hands on heads.
- Sing your instruction to the class.
- Use humour and your good nature to bring children back on task.
- Give instructions that involve standing up, sitting down and turning round.
- Play music to signal stop and go.

Working together

Provide opportunities for the children to spot and report good behaviour. Ask them why they felt it demonstrated the positive ethos of your school and classroom, and allow them the opportunity to reward the child they have chosen. Send children to another class to tell other children how pleased you are with their behaviour. Passing it around school can have a constructive influence on others. Involve the other adults in the class in the reward systems and ask parents to tell you when their child has been well behaved at home. Working together in such a way enables everybody to have an input and allows us to be aware of some of the things we do not always see.

Positive statements

We are good at using these and we know that most children respond well when receiving praise. Have a variety of phrases on hand for different reasons.

- I am really pleased with you because ...

- You have made me very happy today.
- Can you tell everybody why I am so pleased with you?
- That was a lovely thing to say/do/see.
- Thank you for saying that/doing as you were asked/sitting so nicely.
- I have a big smile on my face because ...
- Your parents will be so pleased when I tell them ...
- I would like you to come and sit on the 'champion's chair' because ...

We know that sometimes behaviour can frustrate or present us with challenges. It can become tiring and weigh us down. By having an agreed policy in place to support both you and the children, these frustrations and challenges can be addressed and reduced. Be positive, dwell on what has been a success, talk yourself into a positive frame of mind and share worries with colleagues when you or the children are having a bad day. Accept that a bumpy ride is a rite of passage, but that with the right support and systems in place you can achieve together, and create a harmonious classroom where children thrive under your guidance and support.

KEY POINTS

- Consult with all stakeholders to ensure the message you are delivering about behaviour is consistent, coherent and clear to all involved.
- Ensure your policy is a living document. Do not let it become stagnant, keep it evolving as you grow together.
- Support one another when you face challenges and share ideas to solve problems.
- Plan the principles of the policy into long-, medium- and short-term curriculum plans to establish and embed good behaviour.
- Involve parents in the day-to-day achievements of their child in terms of behaviour.
- Celebrate successes and work together to achieve your goals.
- Be positive!

6 Creative approaches to behaviour management

This chapter is dedicated to examining a wealth of creative ideas, strategies and approaches which can be adopted by teachers in the 'fight against poor behaviour'. It specifically looks at:

- behaviour management strategies for the twenty-first century;
- effective practice linked to peer and self management;
- innovative behaviour management strategies for raising self-esteem.

Revisiting, revising and adapting practice in education cannot be underestimated, particularly when one considers the importance of critical self-analysis and reflection, which all schools are to embrace through the OFSTED (2006a) Self Evaluation Form (SEF). However, for areas of strength to be suitably developed, and weaknesses to be positively addressed, doing 'the same thing but in a different way' is simply not enough; teachers need to consider innovative and exciting strategies and approaches so as to develop the knowledge, skills and understanding required to manage those with the potential to disrupt. We will begin by considering strategies that are being adopted by teachers to manage our twenty-first century children.

Behaviour management strategies for the twenty-first century

Let us draw you straight into some critical reflection by examining what some children might refer to as a 'smelly strategy'!

Aromatherapy

Whilst many may initially be sceptical at the thought of aromatherapy being an effective way to manage children's behaviour, an OFSTED team recognized it in 2006 as an 'innovative approach' when inspecting the provision of a nursery setting in Derbyshire:

The school has also led the way in developing services, including an aromatherapy and massage project and use of the sensory room, to help children remain calm and develop understanding of their own feelings.

(OFSTED 2006b: 4)

To appreciate the potential benefits of using aromatherapy in the classroom it is important for you to be clear about what aromatherapy actually is. What do you personally think aromatherapy is? Compare your response to the details provided below – how does this challenge, enrich or extend your personal knowledge and understanding?

For clarification, we turn to the Aromatherapy Council (2008) which defines aromatherapy as 'the therapeutic use of essential oils ... which are either massaged into the body to be absorbed through the skin, or inhaled by means of vaporisers'. Current thinking among many practitioners, including Womack (2008), in the field of aromatherapy is that scents from the oils stimulate receptors in the nose, which trigger activity in the brain linked to mood and memory. Oils absorbed via the skin into the bloodstream are thought to positively influence the nervous system, mental state and emotions, although as yet there is no concrete or 'good' evidence/research to support this, as highlighted by BUPA (2007).

Aromatherapy is frequently used to relieve stress, headaches, insomnia, tension and pain, and to aid relaxation and general well-being; at present, it is being increasingly used in cancer care and sports therapy. With this in mind, it is likely that you may perceive the use of aromatherapy to be more appropriate for adults, yet it is believed to be suitable for people of all ages, even babies. As a result, a number of schools are beginning to consider using aromatherapy to support children, particularly those with behavioural difficulties.

CASE STUDY

The Cheiron Project, run by the University of Liverpool's Education Department, used aromatherapy as part of its practice in a stress-therapy unit for two Merseyside primary schools, which offered intensive six-week courses in tackling anxiety among children aged between 5 and 11.

Referrals were made to the unit for stress therapy by teachers for any pupils they felt would benefit. Pupils and their families attended the unit (based in the schools' premises) three times a week, with therapies, including hand massage, counselling, psychotherapy and aromatherapy, provided in a setting that used light and music to create a relaxing atmosphere.

Reflecting on the benefits of the therapy, research fellow Bob Spalding said:

Parents are saying that their children are calmer after the therapy and they're more able to talk about their problems. What parents most appreciate is that problems can be dealt with on the spot, without having to make appointments outside the school. This way we can help prevent the chances of behavioural problems developing later.

(BBC 1999)

> **THINK**
>
> - What do you think the views of the teachers were about this unit?
> - What impact do you think this would have on potential learning and teaching in the classroom?
> - What do you consider to be some of the issues with setting up and running a project of this nature in schools you know of? List these. How could you manage and potentially overcome these?

If you are interested in further examining the benefits of using aromatherapy with children, we recommended the work of Solomons (2005) as valuable additional reading. This positive view is held for the benefits for children, particularly those with special education needs and emotional and behavioural difficulties (EBD). But issues linked to training, appropriateness (issues of having close physical contact with children), and the simple logistics of adopting it as standard practice in the primary classroom prevent many teachers from even considering this as an option for behaviour management. However, a number of teachers have taken on board the basic principles of aromatherapy and have introduced scented candles in their classrooms, which they light, and position in high safe places as their children work, whilst others have encouraged children to rub gel sanitizers into the hands of their peers prior to snack or dinnertime.

> **CONSIDERATION**
>
> You may have children in your class who suffer from allergies or asthma – they are likely not to respond positively to the use of aromatherapy as it may trigger rather negative reactions.

Whilst a link between stimulating children's sense of smell and touch and positive behaviour has been noted, most schools are seeing greater dividends when they stimulate children's taste buds.

Healthy eating

With heart disease being found in children as young as 2 years old (National Heart Forum 2007), it is more important than ever before for children to eat healthy and adopt a healthy lifestyle. Evidence shows how certain foods and drinks can have an adverse effect on children's behaviour, as highlighted by the quote below from a parent who was surveyed as part of the Food Commission's (2003) Parents Jury:

> At age 6, my son had a very strong reaction to Sunny Delight, a product I had refused to let him drink since aged about 3, when I noticed the ingredients. After drinking [it], he changed from being a lively yet pleasing and agreeable child, to

one totally unable to calm himself, understand reprimands and respond to direction.

QUESTIONS

- Think about the foods and drinks that were available when you were a child – were there any which you were not allowed? Why was this?
- Consider the different foods and drinks children like to have – which ones are prone to having an adverse effect on behaviour? How do you know this?
- Take a look at some of the ingredients in the food you have in your house – are you surprised/shocked at the contents of these? Why, or why not?

As many schools adopt local, regional and national programmes to effectively embrace the National Healthy Schools agenda, children are now being encouraged, amongst other things, to eat more fruit and vegetables. Drinking plenty of fresh water and partaking in various forms of physical activity both inside and outside of school on a daily basis are also advocated, so that children feel happy, healthy and do better in learning and life. Adopting this initiative accentuates the clear links between children's health, achievement and behaviour – children who have a balanced diet, are well hydrated and consume food and drink with reduced sugar, salt and additive contents are more likely to live longer, achieve more and behave better.

ACTIVITY

Navigate your way through the Healthy Schools website (http://www.healthyschools. gov.uk) paying particular attention to the 'themes'. Take a look at the 'teaching and learning materials' available and consider the value of these in supporting your practice in the classroom in relation to promoting healthy living and good behaviour in the children you teach.

Random resources

In response to the publication, *Excellence and Enjoyment* (DfES 2003c), creativity and interactivity remain high-profile considerations on the educational agenda and, as a result, many teachers are being creative with a range of resources in an attempt to manage children's behaviour. Selected examples of practice are provided below which span the 3–11 age range.

Early Years Foundation Stage – teddy bears

In recognition of the success of Barnaby Bear as part of the QCA's (1999) *Scheme of Work for Geography for Key Stage One and Two*, a number of practitioners in the early years are using teddy bears as an effective way to manage young children's behaviour. This is achieved by introducing 'Ben the behaviour bear' (for example) to the children as a bear who 'looks out' for good behaviour – any child behaving well in the setting is given the privilege of sitting with the bear on the carpet and is the only child who is allowed to touch the bear. For exceptional behaviour the bear may be taken home with the child for the evening/weekend, not only to show the bear how well behaved the child is at home but also give parents/carers a clear indication as to how well their child is behaving in the setting.

CASE STUDY

A setting in the North East of England developed a strategy well received by parents/carers of using teddy bears as a way of comforting children who were distressed by the behaviours of other children. As opposed to directly intervening in response to behavioural issues, children who may have been kicked or teased by others were encouraged to hug and talk to the teddy bear about their feelings and problems. A sympathetic practitioner listened to what was said and put strategies in place to manage these behaviours and feelings under the direction of the bear. Practitioners found that children were more 'open' with the bears and this helped to support children in various aspects of social and emotional aspects of learning, known as SEAL (DCFS 2007).

Key Stage 1 – rest mats

'Children need rest to do their best' is the headline of a campaign led by the National Center on Sleep Disorders Research at the National Heart, Lung, and Blood Institute (NHLBI) in America. Their view is that children all over the world go to school every day deprived of the recommended age-related hours of sleep, which has a real impact on children's abilities to listen, learn and behave. Coupled with the increased pace of daily life (Henderson 2007), it is becoming increasingly important for both adults and children to take moments out of their busy day to rest, thus reducing the effects of stress and anxiety.

CONSIDERATION

Do you know how many hours of sleep the children you teach (and you for that matter) should have per night? Take a look at the interesting work of Saisan *et al.* (2007) to find out.

Whilst an American perspective of this issue is presented, information and ideas associated with it have 'crossed the waters' to the United Kingdom. For example, a number of schools have purchased rest mats (similar to exercise mats) on which children are allowed to lie, doze, power nap, or take time to reflect on their learning during designated short periods of the school day. Teachers in a primary school in the Midlands, who have adopted this approach, play soft music at a low volume, with the lights dimmed and curtains closed to create a calming environment for the children to rest in. They have noted a difference in the children's behaviour, acknowledging how the children seem calmer, refreshed and ready to learn after a short period of time on their mats.

QUESTIONS

- What do you think the teacher does when all of the children are on their mats?
- How long do you think the children have on their mats? How often do you think the children use the mats in this way?
- With many schools struggling to fit all of the curriculum subjects into the school week, what subject areas do you think should be 'rearranged' to accommodate for 'mat time'.

Key Stage 2 – stress balls

The notion that children can suffer from stress remains an interesting and rather surprising revelation for many teachers in primary classrooms today. Studies conducted in Britain, as discussed by Wale-Carole (2000), highlight how many children in today's society suffer with stress because of varied emotional, physical and social factors. Teachers are becoming more aware of the 'symptoms of stress' (particularly as many are unfortunately experiencing them themselves), and so various strategies are being put in place to support those who are experiencing high levels of stress.

ACTIVITY

Take a look at the list of symptoms below and tick off those which you feel may be applicable to children who may be suffering from the effects of stress:

- Difficulty sleeping
- Loss of confidence
- Feeling sick
- Becoming defensive
- Raised heart rate
- Bursting into tears

- Sweaty palms
- Becoming snappy.

Source: adapted from Cowley (2006: 246–7)

Interestingly, all of the symptoms above are indicators of stress. In order to manage these stress levels, particularly during the end of Key Stage Two Standard Assessment Tests (SATs) (see www.satsguide.co.uk/what_are_sats.htm), teachers are giving children stress balls to help relieve their anguish and frustration. Shaped like animals, foods and sports balls, these aids have proved to be a valuable resource in managing the children's behaviour. Alternatives to this include the use of aggression cushions – small colourful cushions which are distributed around the classroom for the children to go and 'punch' when they were feeling frustrated or angry. Balls of Blu-Tack can also be given to the children to play with; this has been noted by some teachers as having a therapeutic effect on the children as they manipulate the material between their fingers.

Calming corners

Classrooms in primary schools are busy places with an abundance of educationally stimulating and interactive learning opportunities on offer. However, for some children, this can be rather overwhelming and teachers now are beginning to appreciate the need for children to actually have some 'down time' – time in which they are able to relax and appreciate the benefits of peace and tranquility in their lives. To embrace this, a number of schools have set up calming corners either in their classrooms or in a designated room in the school in which can be found a range of resources including cushions, magazines and books, music, pictures, nice furniture, lights and small pets to calm and relax children.

SCENARIO

Your head teacher has provided you with some money to create a calming corner in your classroom.

- What would you do to the physical environment to accommodate this corner in your classroom?
- How would you decorate the area so that it oozes peace and tranquility?
- Would you seek the help of children in creating the corner? If so, why? If not, why not?
- Would you teach children how to use it? If so, why? If not, why not?
- When would you allow children to use it?
- How often would you allow children to visit?
- How would you manage what takes place in there?

Whilst the obvious issues surrounding cost and space prevent this being a feature in every school, there are various benefits in terms of managing behaviour, not only for children but also for adults, especially if staff members are allowed to use the facility as well.

Physical activity

The thinking behind this approach to behaviour management is relatively simple: if you want children to behave well just ensure they engage with lots of physical activity. Whilst there are many who already embrace this idea, there are practitioners who question whether it really does help to manage behaviour. The case study below is designed to address this query.

CASE STUDY

A large primary school in the West Midlands unfortunately found itself in special measures and the head teacher knew that she had to find a way of raising standards and improving behaviour, believing raising children's confidence and self-esteem to be the key. By considering various forms of physical activity, the staff developed a gradual programme of activity which introduced whole-school dance sessions, including 'doing the Macarena!', five-minute 'Wake and Shake' bursts of activity, Brain Gym exercises and military-style delivered movement routines before the children entered the school at the start of the day. Physical activity became an integral part of taught sessions in class, where the expectation was for teachers to plan for physical activity throughout lessons, thus reducing the amount of time children were sitting either on the carpet or at their desks.

Training for all staff working with children at playtime and lunchtime was provided, with an emphasis on staff playing *with* the children, teaching them various games and generally interacting with them, rather than just supervising them. Two learning support practitioners and two learning support assistants devised a lunchtime programme including aerobics, skipping, space hoppers, games and other activities, which were supervised. The playground was newly painted and equipped with climbing frames. Staff members were encouraged to run morning, lunchtime and after-school clubs including netball, skipping and short tennis clubs which a mixture of boys and girls attended.

The head teacher is in no doubt that the programme has been worthwhile, and that other schools, even in difficult circumstances, could adopt a similar approach with great results. 'I think it's one of the best things we've ever done in this school: it's not an add-on – it's part of our ethos. It raises standards because it raises self-esteem and behaviour, and the children are focused on learning – it really has been brilliant.'

Source: adapted from TeacherNet (2008).

REFLECT

- What do you think the obstacles are for children and adults getting involved in projects like this?
- If schools are short of money, how might they be able to generate the funding necessary to make projects like this work?
- If you were working at the school which club would you offer to run to promote physical activity? Why?

Playground games

Playtime for most children is an opportunity to have fun with their friends, get valuable exercise and 'blow off a little steam'. However, many teachers find that they have to deal with a number of behavioural difficulties either when they are actually on duty or when their class returns from the playground (Brownhill 2007). This directly influences the ability of the teachers on duty to manage effectively all of those on the playground, and of the teachers back in their classrooms to maximize the amount of time available for learning and teaching with their children. Many behavioural difficulties stem from a lack of things to do – children in Early Years Foundation Stage settings have access to a wealth of resources, including bikes, balls, books, slides, water and sand trays, construction sets and jigsaws, which support and extend the learning that takes place indoors. When many children from Key Stage 1 and 2 classrooms step out onto the playground, they are usually faced with a large grey tarmacked space – and that is it.

THINK

How could the practice of Early Years Foundation Stage settings of providing resources for outdoor learning be translated into the primary playground? Focus your thoughts on the core subjects to begin with. Consider guided writing opportunities on the playground floor with chalk, using hopscotch markings to teach children about double numbers, and playing with bats and balls to put 'forces' into a practical context as initial ideas.

With an 'underlying assumption that the classroom and the playground are intimately connected' (Learning and Teaching Scotland 2007), many schools are adopting a wealth of playground initiatives to make playtime a fun, interesting and valuable time for children. Initiatives include the use of playground games – traditional games played in times gone by that are no longer played as they have been forgotten. By training all staff members to organize and play these games effectively, children are now being introduced to a wealth of simple tag games, ball games, command games, parachute games and skipping songs.

Other initiatives include singing playgrounds and playground peacemakers, which can be developed through links with Playground Partnerships.

EXTENDING YOUR LEARNING

Take a look at Playground Partnerships at http://www.playgroundpartner-ships.org. Consider the implications of their work for supporting you and your school in developing a better playtime for children. Contact your local authority to establish what is going on in your local area linked to singing playgrounds.

Acceptable behaviour contracts

The acceptable behaviour contract is an intervention strategy advocated by the Home Office (http://www.homeoffice.gov.uk) which is designed to support young people and adults in recognizing their antisocial behaviour and its negative effects on others in their community. With its primary goal of stopping offending behaviours, it acts as a contract which clearly identifies the antisocial acts that the offender agrees not to continue with, and stipulates the consequences if any aspect of the agreement is breached, which may include antisocial behaviour orders (ASBOs), evictions and possession proceedings.

CONSIDERATION

Many of you may consider the above not to be applicable to the age range of children you are teaching, yet it is important to acknowledge that the youngest child to date to be the recipient of an ASBO is 10 years old (North 2005), the youngest age at which a child can actually be given an ASBO. You may teach a child in your class who has an ASBO – how will you effectively support the child in school?

Our interest, however, is not in ASBOs but in the way in which the contract is drawn up. Many schools are using the premise of the acceptable behaviour contract to develop their own behaviour management agreements, contracts and action plans, which allows them to clearly document expectations, actions and consequences so that parents, carers, teachers and children clearly understand policy and procedures.

Whilst the idea of using a contract is not necessarily a creative strategy, the way in which these are being developed and shared with others is where the creativity is allowed to 'shine through'. Strategies include:

- uploading examples of contracts onto the school's website, carefully maintaining the anonymity of those involved;
- producing dual-language versions of the contracts;
- producing contracts in consultation with the parents/carers and children so there is some sense of ownership in its content;
- allowing children to sign the contracts along with parents and carers;

- developing simple versions of the contracts which have been made available for young children and adults with low literacy skills, using pictures and digital images to support the text;
- encouraging children to design the format of the contract, considering the most important aspects and how these should be laid out on the page;
- producing DVDs and videos which show practitioners in the school talking through and modelling strategies which have been effective in managing their child's behaviour – these have been particularly useful for parents who need to 'see it to believe it';
- setting up regular review meetings, allowing a triangulation of information to assess progress – teacher in school, parents at home and the child's own personal views both in and out of school.

Behaviour co-ordinators

An interesting development over the last few years relates to the introduction of behaviour co-ordinators in schools. Many of you will be aware of subject co-ordinators who lead core and foundation subject areas across the whole school. The idea of a co-ordinator for behaviour stems from the BECOs scheme, developed in Scotland in 2004, which sets out to train teachers to become behaviour co-ordinators and thus help their colleagues deal with classroom disruption before it has a chance to escalate. BECOs, short for *BE*haviour *CO*-ordinator*s*, adopt what is referred to as a 'staged intervention' approach to behaviour management. This comes in the form of a framework which ensures that sequential phases of behaviour management are followed to combat persistent discipline difficulties. It aims to empower teachers by taking a 'no blame' approach, and supports a problem-solving approach to responding to disruptive behaviour. But what does this framework look like, and what happens in each stage?

ACTIVITY

The following is an example of a staged intervention framework. However, this has been jumbled up and it is your task to consider the points below and decide whether they belong to Level One (L1), Level Two (L2) or Level Three (L3), Level Three being the highest level of intervention. A couple of examples have been done to support you:

- The plan to initiate change is put into action and reviewed at the end of a six-week period. ————
- Outside agencies are now involved in the process and a review of the strategies used to date is undertaken. ————
- The teacher and behaviour co-ordinator jointly plan observations of the behaviour causing concern. **L1**
- The teacher completes an environmental checklist, and at this stage the

focus is on the classroom/learning environment rather than the individual pupil. ————
- Parents/carers are fully involved at this stage. **L3**
- The teacher makes contact with the behaviour co-ordinator to raise issues of concern. The concern is discussed with an agreement of confidentiality. ————
- The teacher and behaviour co-ordinator discuss and construct a plan to initiate change. ————
- At this level an individual behaviour plan for the pupil with clear and specific targets is introduced. ————
- Parents/carers may be involved at this stage. ————
- The individual behaviour plan is put into action and reviewed at the end of a six-week period. ————

Compare your ideas to the answers found at the end of this chapter.

Engaging with this activity will hopefully have made you aware of the importance of approaching behavioural difficulties in a systematic and planned manner. It is also designed to raise your awareness of the importance of environmental checklists and individual behaviour plans as tools for assessment and planning strategies for action.

EXTENDING YOUR LEARNING

You are encouraged to take a look at and potentially use the excellent environmental checklist developed by the Leicestershire County Council Educational Psychology Service which is accessible as a PDF file from http://www.leics.gov.uk/learning_environment_checklist_-_2007_version.pdf. This examines learning environments on different levels, including the class, whole school, and out-of-class.

Similarly, the work of Mortimer (2004) comprehensibly guides readers through the implementation, monitoring and evaluation of individual behaviour plans with suggested recording formats. Whilst this work is early years based, many of the strategies, techniques and approaches are easily adaptable for the primary classroom.

Peer and self-management

It is perfectly normal for many students and teachers who read texts about behaviour management to become somewhat overwhelmed by the enormity of the task ahead of them when they enter a classroom and are expected to manage the behaviour of individuals, small groups of children and the class as a whole. But you do not have to 'go it alone' and it is not, as some teachers perceive it, a sign of weakness, incapability or laziness to consider ways in which others can support you in managing children's behaviour – in fact this is a healthy and effective way of dealing with difficulties. So who can help us to manage children's behaviour? Well, for starters we could ask the children themselves to help us through peer mediation.

Peer mediation is a process in which children's issues of conflict and dispute are effectively managed by their peers. Through elected peer mediators, these issues are dealt with in a calm and supportive manner, allowing all children involved to express their thoughts, feelings and points of view. As non-judgemental facilitators for talk and discussion, peer mediators offer children opportunities to deal effectively with issues and incidents through problem-solving, negotiation and understanding. This approach has been used effectively with children in primary, secondary and special schools.

REFLECT

• From this short introduction to the concept, does this sound like a valuable approach to behaviour management in your setting?
• If so, why? What do you perceive to be the benefits of this approach?
• If not, why not? What do you perceive to be some of the obstacles in developing and sustaining this approach in your setting?

A sequence of process stages, identified by the DfEE (2000) provides a useful structure to the way in which peer mediation is conducted:

1. Define the problem.
2. Identify the key issues.
3. Explore the possible options together.
4. Negotiate a plan of action and agreement.
5. Follow up the outcomes.

As you will clearly see, these stages ideally mirror those taken by teachers in the classroom when dealing with children's behaviour. However, as children are involved in the successful deployment of this process, it is important that:

• the mediator's role is clearly established so that they know which behaviours they are able to manage;
• ground rules are established so that children who work with the mediators know what is acceptable and unacceptable;
• each child is given the opportunity to tell their side of the story without interruption;
• mediators do not pass judgement on what they hear.

Warne (2003) stresses that it is essential that the children involved are asked what they would each like to happen and can see this being done, as and where appropriate. The thinking behind this is that children are more likely to select consequences which are fit for purpose as opposed to having to endure a consequence imposed on them by a teacher who does not truly understand the circumstances surrounding a particular incident, nor the feelings of those involved. Hutchinson and Fannon (2004) are of the opinion that children who devise their own sanctions are more likely to accept them and see them through.

Rogers (2007) provides convincing arguments on the benefits of adopting this approach with individuals, highlighting the potential development of speaking and listening skills, respecting each other's differences and responding more appropriately to issues of conflict and concern (see Rogers 2007: 246–9). However, for peer mediation to work successfully, it needs to be consistently managed by an adult team and requires the support of the entire school community.

> EXTENDING YOUR LEARNING
>
> You are encouraged to engage with the following recommended readings, as detailed on http://www.behaviour4learning.ac.uk, to support your developing understanding of this approach to behaviour management:
>
> Cowie, H. and Wallace, P. (2000) *Peer Support in Action: From Bystander to Standing By*. London: Sage.
> Cremin, H. (2002) Pupils resolving disputes: Successful peer mediation schemes share their secrets. *Support for Learning*, 17(3): 138–43.
> DfEE (2000) *Bullying – Don't Suffer in Silence. An Anti-bullying Pack for Schools*. London: DfEE.
> Warne, A. (2003) Establishing peer mediation in a special school context. *Pastoral Care* (December): 27–33.

This is just one of a number of approaches that involve a child's peers in the management of their behaviour. Schools and settings are becoming increasingly creative in developing strategies and systems which effectively use peer support as a technique for behaviour management. Other strategies include the following:

- peer buddies (Hoy 2004), assigning one or two children to closely monitor the behaviour of a particular child, encouraging them to offer support and gentle direction when necessary;
- peer appraisal (Rogers 2007), allowing children to make an informed judgement on how well a child has behaved during a session or day, based on observation as opposed to personal feelings or preconceived perceptions;
- peer group acceptance (Sell 2004), encouraging the rest of the child's class mates to accept the child for who they are and how they behave, supporting them through both positive and not so positive experiences;
- peer group support (Hoy 2004), setting up a small network of children that a particular child can access to support them when they are misbehaving;

- peer pressure (Cowley 2006), encouraging others to apply gentle pressure so that they model appropriate behaviours for particular children to see as being 'the norm'.

All of these strategies rely on children taking and playing an active and positive role in supporting the behaviour of individuals and groups of children within their class or school. Whilst this is empowering and creditable, it is important to ensure that children do not become 'power crazy', which unfortunately can sometimes happen, and think that they can ultimately manage you, the teacher.

> SCENARIO
>
> A child in your Year 6 class begins to think they are capable of managing the children's behaviour better than you – what would you do?

It may be that the use of peer support strategies is not appropriate in your particular class or school setting due to the nature of the behaviours you are dealing with or the dispositions of the children you teach. With this in mind, a number of teachers have begun to adopt a creative approach to behaviour management which relies on the children managing their own behaviour. This is achieved by teaching them self-management techniques so that they can change and/or maintain appropriate behaviours themselves, thus taking ownership of their actions. The research of Mooney *et al.* (2005) highlights five commonly used self-management interventions:

- Self-monitoring – this involves children observing and recording their own targeted behaviours on a tick sheet.
- Self-evaluation – this is similar to self-monitoring as it involves children's self-assessment and self-recording of behaviour. It also involves comparing their own performance to criteria set by themselves or a teacher – for example, on improving performance over time.
- Self-instruction – this involves children making explicit statements to themselves to direct their own behaviour: 'Sit down, Tommy, and listen!'
- Goal-setting – this requires children to set behaviour targets such as completing a piece of work or interaction with their peers.
- Strategy instruction – this involves teaching children a series of simple steps to follow independently in order to solve a behavioural problem and thus achieve a positive outcome.

But what might this look like in practice?

CASE STUDIES

Self-monitoring. James (5 years old) is asked to make a note of each time he sits on the carpet with his arms folded and his legs crossed. Suzie (10 years old) colours in a square on a chart to indicate that she has pushed her chair underneath her table before she goes out to play.

Self-evaluation. Demi (7 years old) shows her teacher her behaviour chart, which shows an entire row of smiley faces for eating all of her dinner over a two-week period. Sam (9 years old) compares his three days of positive 'green cards' with a target he wrote in his behaviour book to have two full days of green cards.

Self-instruction. Jack (6 years old) mentally reminds himself to go to the toilet before sitting down to start his maths work. Lydia (8 years old) ensures her pencils are all sharp and she has access to an eraser before she settles into her extended writing task.

Goal-setting. Greg (6 years old) sets himself a target to write three complete sentences before the bell rings at 10.15. Wendy (9 years old) aims to work on her science experiment write-up for 10 minutes without talking to anyone around her.

Strategy instruction. Mrs Holder teaches her Year 1 class how to use deep breathing techniques to calm themselves down as opposed to lashing out at others with their fists. Mr Jackson talks his Year 4 class through strategies he used when he was a boy to cope when being bullied.

REFLECT

At the end of their study, Mooney *et al.* pose the following questions on the implications of their research for practitioners which we would like you to consider:

- What formal or informal self-management techniques do you already use with your children, and how could they be further developed in light of the findings from this study?
- Could these techniques be used in whole-class teaching?

In order to answer these it is beneficial for you to read the research paper, the details of which are provided in the References section at the back of the book.

Challenging the creative approach

Whilst many teachers are keen to find and use new strategies to manage children's behaviour, there is a strong research base (OFSTED 2005) which argues convincingly that schools can reduce behaviour issues in a reasonably short time if they use a range of tried and trusted methods – simple strategies which, if applied consistently by everyone, will have the desired effect:

- Provide children with a clear choice – either they do X or Y.
- Look for the good in children and their behaviour.
- Empathize but do not settle for anything less than your high expectations (Brownhill 2007).
- Avoid losing your temper in front of children.
- Smile!
- Be firm but fair.
- Make sure children know it is their behaviour you are displeased with and not the child.
- Provide stimulating activities for all children to engage with.
- Ensure all children are suitably challenged (Docking and McGrath 2002).
- Make children feel good about themselves.
- Be consistent (Dix 2007).
- Give advice to children before giving them warnings (Hook and Vaas 2006).
- Say what you mean and mean what you say.
- Shower children in positive praise.
- Have clearly defined class and school rules. Refer to these regularly (Kyriacou 2002).
- Catch children being good.
- Be a good role model – show them the behaviours that you want to see in them.
- Use visual stimuli and resources to manage and reward behaviours – stickers, images, stamps, cards, badges and pictures.

As we have already discussed in Chapter 2, there are many reasons why children misbehave, but, as research has proved, most behavioural difficulties stem from low self-esteem (Kamen 2003). As schools strive to build the self-esteem of the children they work with, teachers are continually calling out for new and innovative strategies to support this. So, in true creative fashion, here are several different strategies which you can dip into, use and adapt as effective practice in your own classroom:

- Put images of the child's work on the home page of the school website.
- Allow the child to use the class's/school's IPod/MP3 player.
- Allow the child to sit on at the 'top table' in class – a chair and table designated for 'brilliant' children. Only one child is allowed to sit at it at any one time. Some teachers allow the 'brilliant' child to sit at their desk.
- Allow children to sit and eat their dinner with the teachers in the dinner hall.

Some schools allow brilliant children to eat their dinner in the staffroom. For excellent behaviour, the head teacher in one school in the South of England takes these children out for a meal with the children's parents.

- Allow children to be school ambassadors. When visitors or prospective parents come to the school, these children are permitted to come out of class and show them around, talking to the parents/visitors about the school and answering questions where appropriate.
- Allow children's work to be displayed in public places in the locality in leisure centres, libraries and town halls.
- Build in visits from people in the local community to personally congratulate the child – vicars, chair of governors, local councillors.

TOP TIPS

- Send letters home, providing details on the wonderful behaviour of particular children – parents/carers adore this sort of practice.
- Make phone calls to parents/carers along with text messages using the school's mobile phone – parents usually expect to hear bad news when they get a call or a message from school! A school in the North-West of England allows children to telephone their parents from school, informing them about how pleased their teacher is with their behaviour. This only really works, however, if the parents are at home to take the call.
- Include images of well-behaved children in displays of pictures of staff members in the school. Display boards with headshots of teachers, teaching assistants, midday supervisors, cleaning staff and governors, including images of well-behaved children who are displayed under the title 'the brilliantly behaved faces of ———— Primary School'.
- Allow children to select the music which is played every day when the children enter and exit the hall for daily acts of worship/assembly. Obviously, checks should be made to ensure the music is not too rowdy or full of inappropriate language!
- Allow one 'star' child to sit at the front of the hall and watch as the rest of the school come into assembly. The children coming in have to mirror the behaviour of this child.
- Put brilliant children's names on the screensavers on the computers in the classroom, in the ICT suite and on the teacher's computer connected to the Interactive Whiteboard/SMART board.

Use the screensaver strategy when you have open days and parents' evenings – we have seen parents reduced to tears when they see their child's name bouncing around the computer screen indicating that their son/daughter is well behaved.

- Use well-behaved children to be reception monitors, manning the desk and answering the phone when the bursar/secretary goes for their lunch. Train children to answer the phone, undertake tasks, take down messages, call teachers and log jobs to support the smooth running of the school.
- Provide a special common room for well-behaved children to use. By using money obtained through parent friend association fundraising, a school in Wales has taken a room, which used to be a storage cupboard, and decorated and furnished it with attractive chairs, tables and bright decor. Pinball machines, board games and table football games have been provided so that children who are well behaved get the opportunity to use the room under peer supervision. Children are responsible for the maintenance of the room, dusting and tidying up after themselves in preparation for the children who use it next.
- Allow well-behaved children to be the guest editor of the school's newsletter.
- Allow children to lead their own dinner/after-school club (with supervision from a teacher).
- Allow children to take framed pieces of work home (plastic, not glass, please!).
- Allow children to wear the special coat/hat/sash of the school.
- Allow children to tell the *teachers* what to wear on non-school uniform day.
- Allow the children to write the prayer or thought for the day.

KEY POINTS

- Effective behaviour management can simply be a result of stimulating children's senses.
- Adapt the use of everyday resources in the classroom to manage children's behaviour creatively.
- The importance of physical activity cannot be underestimated in successfully managing children's behaviour.
- Peer mediation and self-management strategies are valuable additions to any class teacher's behaviour management 'toolbox'.
- Strive to 'think outside the box', tweaking and playing around with tried and tested strategies so that with a 'creative spin' you can promote good behaviour in your classroom.

ACTIVITY ANSWERS (See pages 112 and 113.)

Level 1:
- The teacher makes contact with the behaviour co-ordinator to raise issues of concern. The concern is discussed with an agreement of confidentiality.
- The teacher and behaviour co-ordinator jointly plan observations of the behaviour causing concern.
- The teacher completes an environmental checklist, and at this stage the focus is on the classroom/learning environment rather than the individual pupil.
- The teacher and behaviour co-ordinator discuss and construct a plan to initiate change.
- The plan to initiate change is put into action and reviewed at the end of a six-week period.

Level 2:
- At this level, an individual behaviour plan for the pupil with clear and specific targets is introduced.
- Parents/carers may be involved at this stage.
- The individual behaviour plan is put into action and reviewed at the end of a six-week period.

Level 3:
- Outside agencies are now involved in the process and a review of the strategies used to date is undertaken.
- Parents/carers are fully involved at this stage.

Source: adapted from MacKay (2004).

7   Using the arts to guide behaviour

This chapter looks at the arts as a vehicle for helping children to understand themselves and their behaviour. We will focus specifically on:

- culture and the arts, and what they mean in practice;
- music and how it can be used to develop self-concept;
- drama and story-telling to enable young people to consider the choices they make and to understand why others sometimes behave inappropriately;
- dance – aesthetics and appreciation for regulation of behaviour;
- art – using pictures, colours and the environment to help children understand their feelings.

Introduction

In recent years, with a greater emphasis on basic skills and meeting targets, children are exposed more and more to the core subjects and less to the arts curriculum. As a result, fewer children have an appreciation of the arts and we as teachers find it increasingly difficult to make room for them, given the other pressures in the curriculum. How do we use the arts to enable children to behave well? This chapter will focus on music, dance, drama and art in relation to behaviour management and children's thinking, feeling and actions and how these can be developed to promote good behaviour in school.

Firstly, let us consider how the arts can generally help us with our behaviour management of pupils in school. According to Bruner (1990), children show an astonishingly strong predisposition to culture and are eager to adopt the folkways they see around them. One of the problems we encounter in school is that many of the children we teach are not part of a common culture, or more frequently, do not understand what their role is in that culture. As a result, we often find that children do not behave as we would wish because they are pushing the boundaries of the culture in order to understand how it works and how they fit within it.

Young learners are people in families and communities, struggling to reconcile their desires, beliefs and goals with the world around them. Children come to appreciate that they are not acting directly on the world but on the beliefs they hold about that world, and this is a gradual process (Bruner 1990). When children come into school, they are often asked to hang up their 'home' coat and put on their 'school' coat, leaving at the classroom door all that rich learning that takes place beyond the realms of the school grounds.

You might ask what this has to do with the arts. The arts themselves hold within each discipline their own culture, where children can apply their feelings, beliefs and understanding in a common place. They can explore how they feel about a painting or a piece of music. They can consider the effect of their actions on others and of others' actions on them and begin to understand the consequences of behaviour in relation to the world around them. This is not necessarily possible through teaching subject knowledge and skill development, but can be explored through narrative, drama and emotional understanding. The culture of school, family and community, which children can build barriers between, can begin to make sense when they are brought together in a way that encourages self-belief and perceptive knowledge of the people, places and behaviours to be found in and around that culture.

The arts play an important part in all our lives, often without us even realizing it. We do not have to take part in any art form for the arts to have an impact on our lives. Most of us listen to music, many of us go to shows or visit exhibitions, some of us participate by playing a musical instrument, acting, dancing or painting. As teachers, we recognize the importance of the arts in the curriculum and regret that there seems little time for class/school plays, experimenting with musical instruments or going out to sketch, take photographs and paint images we have seen. However, there is time, if we believe the arts to be of enough importance and enable children to link their learning in the arts to other curriculum areas and their lives beyond the classroom.

Education is a major embodiment of a culture's way of life, not just a preparation for it. Individual societies and cultures have expressed their deepest beliefs and feelings through music, art, dance and story. Studying the arts enables people to understand and appreciate individuals, communities and cultures and, as a result, we enable young people to develop as responsible citizens who are sensitive to the beliefs and practices of others, and this is why the arts are so important for behaviour management.

One of the things we particularly like about the arts is the way in which they encourage resilience and perseverance. When did you last learn a new skill from scratch? Can you read basic music notation, learn a dance or master an artistic technique? How much perseverance and tolerance does it take to learn a new skill? How does it make you feel once you have mastered the skill? This learning involves discipline, time and diligence, provides children with the opportunity to feel good about themselves, learn what self-efficacy means, and builds self-esteem, all helping to fight the battle against poor behaviour.

Music

Fisher (2003: 232) says that 'music binds us in a special way to our social and cultural context'. He believes that that it is a unique tool for arousing our physical, emotional and intellectual faculties. Because of this, music is an ideal tool for managing behaviour because of its use of active listening skills, which are essential in our everyday lives.

Music can be used in many ways to enable children to behave well and to consider their behaviour in relation to their mood. It can also be used to create moods and atmospheres in the classroom that you consider appropriate for a given activity. You can use music to set a tone, maintain noise levels, and encourage concentration, independence and responsibility.

ACTIVITY

Select a piece of music that is calm and quiet, for example *La Mer* by Debussy. Elicit from the children their emotional response and encourage them to think about the way in which the music affects their mood.

Do the same with a piece of music that is quite different in its mood, for example *A Night on Bald Mountain* by Mussorgsky. Choose something that is more aggressive in nature. Again, elicit the emotional responses from the children and ask them to think about how they feel when they are listening to the music.

Make a bank of the vocabulary the children produce and encourage them to think about how these words relate to their mood, behaviour and actions towards one another. This can be done as a circle time activity. You might ask questions like the following:

- Feel the pulse of the music. How does this relate to the way your heart beats? Is there a difference in the way your heart beats from the first piece of music? What does this tell you about yourself?
- How does the music make you feel?
- What does the music do to your mood?
- Which piece of music makes you feel more able to work together in a collaborative way?
- How can the words you have given relate to the way in which you behave towards one another?

THINK

Following your discussion of the music and the children's responses to each piece, ask them to consider how the music might help them when they are faced with a confrontation. Encourage them to create statements that relate to the calm feelings from the word bank they have developed.

- How might you link these activities into the everyday aspects of your classroom?
- How might you enable children to think about their feelings and connect them to the music to prevent them from having aggressive physical encounters during playtime?

Music can also be used in a variety of other ways to encourage good behaviour.

TOP TIPS

How many of the activities listed below do you already use? How many could you incorporate into your routine to manage behaviour in your classroom?

- Coming and going.
  Play calm music as the children enter the room, greet them with a quiet voice to set the tone for the day. Send them out to play with something more lively.

- Whistle while you work.
  Play a piece of music quietly in the background while the children are working. If the children cannot hear the music, they should regulate their noise levels. Ask them to be responsible for monitoring the music.

- Music and routines.
  Associate specific music with particular routines: the *Mission Impossible* theme tune for tidying up, Holst's *Planets* for getting changed for PE.

- Musical moods.
  Play music that is appropriate for the activity. Music that is calm for walking to the carpet or something more lively for a shake-up if the children are restless on the carpet.

- Musical reward.
  When the children have behaved well, reward them by playing a favourite pop tune or piece of music. Use music that the children have brought in from home.

- Rhythm rules.
  If you need to gain the attention of the whole class, clap a rhythm and ask the children to copy it. Once you have done this a few times it should become routine and you can do it without using your voice.

In order to encourage children to begin to understand each other and to become tolerant of difference it is important that they are provided with opportunities to express their musical tastes. By doing so, children may come to understand why people have different musical tastes.

Many children are exposed to music at home that is a cultural or religious choice; we can provide opportunities at school to widen these experiences and expose children to the cultures of others by playing a wide variety of music in the classroom.

On a rolling programme, ask the children to select a piece of music that expresses the music they listen to or are exposed to at home. Once they have selected their piece of music, ask them to consider a number of questions like the following:

- Why did you choose this particular piece of music?
- When is it normally played at home?
- Why is this music played in your home?

- How does it make you feel?
- Does it remind you of anything in particular?
- When you listen to this music, what pictures come into your mind?
- Do you have any memories associated with this piece of music?
- What do you like/dislike about this music and why?

Children can provide a short presentation to their peers once they have prepared their responses. The same activity may also be carried out with music of choice. Of course, it is understood that when music is being played in school you will need to listen to the piece first to ensure the lyrics are appropriate. You may also have to be sensitive to parents' wishes and consider what they deem to be appropriate for their children.

> CONSIDERATION
>
> - How does this type of activity enable children to understand one another?
> - In what ways does it encourage tolerance?
> - How might you encourage all children to participate?
> - What does this do for a child's understanding of their identity?
> - Consider how it enables them to respond to and understand their culture.
> - In what ways do children build self-knowledge as a result?

Drama and story-telling

The use of drama to explore emotions and feelings is not unique to schools. Businesses, hospitals and the police all use role-play and scenarios in order to develop their understanding of the issues they deal with on a day-to-day basis. It is widely used by drama therapists to enable families to examine their actions and words by the use of story, often using traditional tales as a stimulus. Traditional tales are a regular feature in the curriculum and are often explored in terms of character profiles, use of vocabulary and structure.

Story is an implicit part of our culture, and through using narrative we express our most cherished beliefs, our feelings and our understanding of the society in which we find ourselves. Through drama, we can discover our feelings in relation to a wide range of behaviours, including bullying, isolation and abuse. Most importantly, we can do this at a safe distance where we disconnect ourselves from the reality whilst still applying the learning to real-life events.

Children are able to consider the actions of others, can learn strategies for situations in which they may find themselves and learn how their own words and conduct may have consequences for the future. This learning is active learning, which in itself is a good strategy for behaviour management, as by being involved in a structured, well-prepared lesson there is little time to misbehave. It does mean learning the basics to start with by teaching and learning a range of dramatic conventions such as freeze framing, simulation, thought tracking, mantle of the expert and constructing simple scenes.

In order to get the most from any drama session, using the children's ideas and worries provides ownership and responsibility and can therefore be more productive; because it comes from the children they are more likely to make it successful.

As Bolton and Heathcote (1999) remind us, exploring some sensitive issues can often perpetuate the very behaviour you are working to eradicate or are trying to understand. It may be necessary to work in a non-naturalistic form, so that children are not asked to re-enact a series of events that may have happened to them. By placing some distance between the event and the activity it is possible for the children to reflect on the issues in a safe environment where they do not feel threatened.

Before you start to think about using drama with the children you teach, you may like to think about the individuals in your class. It may be that there are particular underlying problems or issues that you may not have fully thought about which could have an effect on the day-to-day behaviour in the setting.

> REFLECT
>
> - What are the relationships in your classroom like?
> - Have you examined the power status within the group?
> - How do you group the children?
> - Do these groups work collaboratively?
> - Do children understand the meaning and language of collaboration?
> - Are there children who find it difficult to find their voice?
> - Are there children who assert their ideas, needs, wishes to others, including you?
> - What do you do to ensure all children have equality of opportunity?

Once you have established these you will have a better idea of how your children work together and the ways in which you can ensure that all children have an opportunity to be heard and valued within the different groups in which they work and in whole-class scenarios.

Now you can get to work on some drama activities to encourage good behaviour and to enable children to develop a better understanding of one another and the world in which they live.

> ACTIVITY
>
> Take a traditional story/tale with a theme that exemplifies good and bad behaviour. Try 'Hansel and Gretel' or 'The billy goats gruff' for example. You do not have to try to act out the story. In fact, we would discourage this as this may influence children to behave in the ways of particular

characters. Note that in drama work in school we say that we are 'working in role' as opposed to 'acting'. Instead, the children are in the role of a forensic scientist or a police officer. You will need to prepare A4 envelopes – each containing the same information. These should be clues from the story. Label the envelopes with a statement such as 'Property of the Police. Contents not to be touched by hand'. Depending on the age of the children you teach, these can be as simple/visual/complex as you deem appropriate.

For 'Hansel and Gretel' you may want to use any or all of the following – or none – go with what you think!

- A picture or map of a forest
- A recipe for gingerbread
- A diary extract from the step mother or father
- Bread
- Twigs
- Feathers
- A picture (or a symbol) of a boy and a girl.

Make these look old, scrunch the paper, discolour with tea and tear each clue so the children have to put them back together. Provide each group with tweezers and magnifying glasses for handling the clues.

In role, explain that you are the detective in charge of the investigation and that you have questioned two children recently about an experience they have had, but you are unable to get the full story. Using the clues available, can they provide a story that might help the police?

Allow time for the building and telling of the story and then ask the children to present their story to the class.

Following the stories, reveal the source of the story and use the following questions to explore the story in more depth:

- Why do you think people sometimes hurt each other?
- What hurts more, physical or emotional hurt? Why?
- How do you think the children felt when they were alone in the forest?
- How did they help each other?
- How was the story resolved?
- Were you happy with the ending?
- How might you change the story to ensure no one is harmed?

REFLECT

- How do these situations and characters link to the lives of the children we teach?

- Not every real-life story ends 'happily ever after' – how do we enable children to identify with these experiences?
- How can you use these opportunities to enable children to understand that the world is not a bad place, but that it is not always kind either?
- How might you encourage the children to make a positive contribution?

In recent times, there have been calls to ban stories that do not have happy conclusions or where the characters suffer. Whilst we do not suggest that all the stories you explore with your class should have unhappy, dark themes, we do encourage thought for those children whose lives are less happy. We do feel it is important that these children be provided with some opportunities to identify with characters whose lives may reflect their own in some way. Drama is an ideal vehicle for this type of exploration.

Try some of the following in an effort to help all children in your class to make the right choices and behave well.

TOP TIPS

- Change events/endings in stories ensuring characters have the opportunity to turn around their bad luck. Apply these strategies to real life where possible.
- Use hot seating to encourage children to see points of view from different characters.
- Create collaborative and caring situations in a role-play area – for example, taking care of plants/babies/friends.
- Use freeze frames to create scenes from stories that explore feelings and moods at a given point and the effect of these on the different characters.

Dance

Dance as art shares the characteristics of other forms of art such as painting, poetry, music and drama. It could be argued that there are two types of *feelings* associated with dance – those that are expressed within the theme of the dance and those that are connected to the creative process of composing or choreographing dance or movement (Smith-Autard 2002). This would suggest that there are both cognitive and expressive processes involved. In relation to behaviour management, children can be encouraged to consider their feelings and to express them through movement. This process of composing movement for the purpose of expression can be useful in regulating aggression, developing self-esteem and making children feel good about themselves.

In terms of expressing themes, dance can also be considered for helping children to understand how their body and mind respond to music, emotions and moods. It can engage them in a powerful process that enables them to develop control, a deeper appreciation of the feelings of others and an understanding of the impact of mood and emotion on their lives generally.

In all art forms, aesthetic education is fundamental. Aesthetic education is essentially an education of feeling. 'In the aesthetic qualities of a work of art we receive an experience of the feelings embodied' (Smith-Autard 2002: 33). Essentially this means that when we listen to a piece of music we respond to it through our emotions. Some music can make us feel sad or happy, a painting may evoke a memory or a picture in the mind, and in dance we may feel a connection with a mood or a theme.

By exposing young people to a range of dance opportunities, we can enable this aesthetic education to flourish. When we consider our own feelings about dance it might be that the first thing we think of is country dancing in the school hall, having to hold hands with a boy or girl and being subjected to the same tunes over and over again. It is important to consider what we are expecting our young people to engage with in terms of dance.

CONSIDERATION

If behaviour management is an issue during a dance lesson, it may be prudent to consider the following:

- The subject or the style of the dance – is it appropriate for the age and interests of the children?
- The groups – have you grouped the children well? We often group the whole class in twos, threes or fours – how about having different size groups throughout the activity: some in groups of two, some in threes, fours and fives. It is not necessary for everybody to be grouped the same and the work produced is much more varied as a result. For other ideas linked to groupings see Chapter 6 (102).
- The music or the stimulus – use something that the children will engage with – country dancing is great when danced to 'Dancing in the Moonlight' by Toploader or 'Moving on Up' by M People.
- Your own response to dancing – how do you present yourself, not only in terms of appropriate dress but also in terms of your enthusiasm, attitude and body language?

Highly skilled teachers in any curriculum discipline have mastered the skills of communication. Within dance, there is also a need to master the skills of physical communication, which apply in a very different way to those communication skills used in a classroom setting.

These teachers demonstrate high energy, to enable young people to mirror their enthusiasm and get up and go. They use open and giving body language, enabling children to respond positively. They consider how they move, sometimes being purposely physically awkward so that children will take the helm and teach them (see http://www.usa-gymnastics.org).

Because dance requires children to listen to their bodies, to be aware of the space in which they move and to make a response to stimuli it encourages concentration, attention and self-awareness. It is essential that we provide young people with the opportunity to build self-awareness. One way to do this is to use movement analysis.

ACTIVITY

Encourage the class to consider the following questions:

What
What is the body doing at a given time?
What are the movements like?
Are they large or small?
Do they follow a pattern?
Do different parts of the body have to work in time together?

Where
What is the space in which the body is working?
How does the movement affect the space?
Is the space appropriate?
Does the given space have an impact on the movements available?

How
How is the body moving?
What is the quality of the movement?
Is the body soft or stretched?
Can the body change the quality of movement in order to interpret a theme or emotion more effectively?

Who
What relationships are important in this dance?
Individual work, pair work, group work, whole class?
How does the space used affect the relationships within the dance?

How does movement analysis enable children to consider other people? How does it encourage children to feel good about themselves? Are they aware of the what, where, how and who? Teamwork and collaboration are important elements of any dance lesson. These two elements require thought, listening to others and developing ideas based on discussion of basic skills for learning to work together and for enabling good behaviour.

How do the following enable teamwork?

- How well children demonstrate their understanding of and interpretation of themes in a dance.
- How small groups make decisions about the type of dance and about the style.
- The way in which children approach the exploration of movement ideas, discovering actions, qualities and spatial features to express the theme.
- How well the children understand the way in which the music or accompaniment can be used to link to their ideas.

Behaviour in the dance lesson

Of course, an important part of a successful lesson is feeling confident about dealing with behaviour that occurs during the lesson. Take a moment to reflect on the types of disruptive behaviour you have experienced while teaching dance.

ACTIVITY

Over the course of the next few lessons you teach, make a note of the different behaviours that occur. Consider the ways in which they disrupt other children, your teaching and the learning that is taking place. List the behaviours and consider the way in which you deal with these.

Look at the table below. How many of these behaviours occur in your lessons? How might the solutions enable behaviour to improve?

The strategies are adapted from Kassing and Jay (2003).

Behaviour	Response	Example
Noise – this is often a problem in any PE lesson, but in dance it is disruptive, counter-productive and unhelpful.	Make your expectations explicit – talking is permitted to organize activities and discuss ideas, but work should be carried out without chatter.	'Remember to express yourself with your movement, not your voice.' Remind children when their voices are too loud.
Giggling during performance – this could be the performers and the audience.	Allow them to laugh to help them stop laughing. By trying too hard to suppress the laughter, you will end up with a worse problem and the concentration will be lost.	'That's OK, now gather your thoughts and focus on the dance please.'
	Children who laugh at their peers should be reminded that this is disrespectful and insensitive.	'Laughing at a funny dance is fine, but please don't laugh at someone else's efforts. You will soon be performing your piece.'
Collisions – sometimes the children become over-excited and their enthusiasm is directed in the wrong way.	Ensure the children are working in their own spaces. Use a predetermined 'freeze' or other sign to stop all action.	'And freeze. Everybody bring your arms to your sides, stand still and look this way.' Carry out some gentle breathing exercises to redirect energies.

Chaos – this occurs when what you are doing is simply not working. This may be due to the activity being inappropriate.	Stop the lesson. Ask everybody to sit down and then move on to another activity.	'Let's move on to the next activity.'
It could be because you have not placed enough structure into the lesson.	Place some 'frames' around the work to provide a structure.	'Create three movements that link together with a bend or a turn to show sadness.'
'I don't want to...' – non-participation can occur when children feel threatened by the situation.	This can often resolve itself by allowing the child to join in when they feel ready.	'When you're ready come and join us.' 'We really need you, will you come and dance with us?'
It may also transpire when the children have little interest in the activity.	Lack of interest can be solved through dialogue with the child and by planning activities that incorporate their ideas and interests.	Ask the children to come up with ideas for the lesson.

Organization, pace and time management are all factors that can make or break any lesson. In the context of dance, these are fundamental elements for success. Good organization creates feelings of safety for the children; they feel secure in the knowledge that you are 'in control', that you have planned well and that you are confident in the lesson material. They are more likely to focus and stay on task when the structure is tight. Therefore, you will need to think about every step of the lesson from the moment the children enter the hall to the moment they make their exit.

- Ensure that before entering the hall the children are clear about your expectations for their behaviour. Talk to the children about noise, contact and listening. Help them to uphold messages of health and safety so that you can be sure that they understand what is expected of them. Present to the children choices for behaviour, make clear the rewards and consequences and explain how these will be followed up in the lesson.
- Provide children with an activity for when they first come into the dance space: 'Find a space and make a small shape, make your body as small as you can.' Use this as the start of your warm-up so that you have a smooth transition into the lesson.
- Once the lesson begins, plan for a range of 'frames' that provide short bursts of activity for all the children. This is a simple way of getting the most out of the lesson, where the children create short phrases of movement that build in small

stages. Remember to plan in opportunities for individual, pair and group work to maintain interest and concentration.

- Do not allow an activity to go on too long. The children will lose their concentration, and that is where the disruptive behaviour often begins. Keep the lesson to a tight timeframe so that you have pace, energy and enthusiasm throughout, and the children are actively thinking and learning, with little time to disrupt others or lose focus.
- During performances, provide children with self and peer assessment opportunities to give them a focal point for the presentation. Ask them to look for specific moments, actions, and messages that they see expressed through the movement. Use these later for discussion purposes when assessing and evaluating the work carried out.
- At the end of a lesson in the 'cool-down', provide children with a simple activity that requires stillness and control, both mentally and physically. This will prepare them for going back to the classroom environment quietly and orderly. As you walk around the space, give a nod or a wink to signal lining up at the door. Do not let this take too long; once the majority of the class have lined up signal to the final few to join the line and make your exit with pace and purpose, maintaining the control and stillness observed in the final activity.

A positive learning atmosphere is conducive to learning and effective teaching and management of the class. Know the boundaries and expectations before you start the lesson. It is easier to set these in advance than to try to incorporate and adjust them later. A firm set of guidelines will enable you to teach rather than just manage or survive the lesson.

Art

As with music, dance and drama, art is an area of the curriculum for exploration in terms of allowing children to understand themselves and others. It allows for 'intersubjectivity' – the human ability to understand other people's minds through language, gesture or other means (Bruner 1990). In this context, it means that children can develop understanding through use of colour, light and works of art. We will also explore ways in which we might manage behaviour in the lesson.

Art connects us to another life (Fisher 2003). It requires us to make a personal response and so challenges our thinking, our ideas and our feelings. Some of these remain internal but others can be shared. Through sharing we are able to regulate, refine and adjust our understanding: 'we can see more when we are helped to see through the eyes and work of others' (Fisher 2003: 228).

Art in the primary school is often devalued, not because we do not want to do it, but because we feel we do not have enough time to explore it properly. It takes a long time to set it up, to clear away and it takes longer than 30 minutes or an hour to really embed and entrench children in the activity. Sometimes there is an anxiety linked to teaching it because we feel deskilled, or not knowledgeable enough about the artists, techniques and history of art. These anxieties can transpose themselves on to the children, which can create nervousness and consequently anxiety in them, which may result in poor behaviour. It is worth remembering that we do not have to be brilliant artists to teach a good art lesson, but being confident is half the battle.

The environment

Colour is very emotive; it produces feelings inside us of which we are often unaware. Think about rooms you have been in where you feel uncomfortable and those rooms where you feel relaxed and peaceful. Those feelings can be formed because of something as simple as the colour the room is painted.

Now consider your classroom. What colour is the paint on the walls, what are the colours used in displays? We suspect that your classroom is a vibrant, buzzing place that creates feelings of excitement and energy, but do the colours direct those energies in the right way? We are not suggesting that you repaint the room, or that you use sombre colours for display, but that you consider how the colours may affect the mood of the pupils. Use red, but not too much, back pictures in red rather than having a red background, use greens, yellows and blues to maintain harmony and stillness. In Scandinavian countries, there has been a move towards using natural materials in educational environments to enable children to feel at one with nature.

Ensuring that the environment is appropriate is important; it enables children to settle quickly and to concentrate their efforts into their work.

Using works of art for behaviour management

We talked before about the necessity to provide opportunities to engage children in thinking about art and the ways that art can help children to understand their lives and those of others, as well as the ideas of the artist as they created the picture. It could be said that the art is created twice, once by the artist and again by the audience as they interpret the picture in their own mind.

ACTIVITY

Take a picture that you are studying or use one like L.S. Lowry's *Industrial Landscape* (1944). Give the children time to look at the picture and to talk about it in small groups. Give them paper and pencils to make any notes or write down any questions. Do this informally. Sharing your beliefs and feelings about paintings can be a very personal point in time, and children may feel vulnerable. Allow them to formulate their ideas and feelings in their own time and to share these if and when they feel ready.

Whilst we sometimes probe children to find out what they are thinking, it is not always necessary or appropriate to do so. Let them keep hold of their personal thoughts too. You will, however, want to stimulate thought and responses to the painting in order to help the children to understand it.

The children can respond in different ways. You know your children – do it in a way that suits them as learners and as people. Below are some suggestions for questions you might ask. This can be done verbally or you might put questions in envelopes or on cards.

- What do you know about this picture by looking at it?
- What do you think about this picture?
- What would you like to know about the picture?
- What story does this picture tell?
- How does it reflect your ideas about life?
- What elements of the picture help you to understand the story better?
- What do you think about when you look at the people and the buildings?
- What might life be like for people living here?
- How does this compare with where you live?
- What have you learned about other people?

REFLECT

- How did the children respond?
- What connections did they make to their home life, parents/guardians, and ideas of the world?
- Did the children discuss their ideas together?
- How well did they collaborate?
- What did they learn about each other?
- Did any of the responses surprise you in anyway?
- What have you learned about the class?

Use artwork to stimulate discussion to enable children to develop their emotional understanding. Choose work that demonstrates a feeling or a mood, where the subjects present a particular emotion. *Amor, Lichtspiele*, by George Grosz (1924), depicts a street scene with a range of characters who have different facial expressions suggesting their feelings at that point in time. The effects and experiences of World War I traumatized Grosz and often provided the material for his paintings, particularly the use of colour, distorted images and the faces he presents in his work. This knowledge of artists is a useful discussion point for understanding how to transpose feelings and experiences into pictures and paintings. You do not have to learn too much, but find out some practical information to enable you to help the children.

Above Lake Superior, by Lawren Harris (1922), is in contrast calm, stark and simple. Comparing paintings and talking about the feelings they inspire can help us to appreciate, identify with and recognize the different feelings we express and display in a range of circumstances. Sometimes children, particularly young children, lash out with physical aggression simply because they do not know how else to express themselves.

When it comes to helping children to develop independence and responsibility our best hope is to enable them to understand the consequences of their behaviour, the effect they have in group situations and how they make themselves and others feel.

By understanding what reaction a feeling or emotion might invoke in themselves, children can learn to regulate and modify their behaviour so that they react in a more appropriate manner. This may be as simple as removing themselves from the situation. Exploring how we feel through works of art can be a rich and rewarding experience and enables us to challenge and adjust behaviour in a creative and profound way.

KEY POINTS

- Providing opportunities to learn about ourselves can help children learn about and understand the culture in which they live.
- Match activities to the needs of the pupils.
- Help children to develop a sense of self through their responses to music, dance, story and art.
- Explore the responses and feelings evoked by art forms to develop a sense of identity and to understand why feelings affect behaviour.

8 Behavioural partnerships

The focus of this penultimate chapter examines the notion of behavioural partnerships in developing good behaviour in the children we work with. It specifically addresses:

- partnerships within the school environment;
- working with parents and carers;
- building partnerships with the local community;
- *Every Child Matters* – initiating and sustaining involvement with multi-agency professionals;
- weighing up the pros and cons of working in partnership with others.

As previously discussed in Chapter 6, the idea of the teacher being the only 'key' (Weber 1982; OFSTED 1999a) to managing behaviour in the classroom is a misconception; thinking in this way inevitably results in many teachers falling ill as they try in vain to deal effectively with every behaviour incident which presents itself. Whilst the use of peer and self management strategies (pages 28 and 29) goes some way to 'sharing out the load', we need to extend this by considering why many teachers and schools are becoming wise to the 'power' of partnerships. By doing so, they are thus reaping the benefits of better behaviour by establishing links and connections with others, both inside and outside the classroom. You may be inclined to ask why these partnerships are so beneficial to schools, teachers and children, and so we will use this question to initiate our discussion of this topic.

Why partnerships?

The concept of partnerships in education is an important factor in ensuring improvements in schools, not only in the quality of provision, but also in raising standards in children's attainment and behaviour. The DCSF (2008) claim that successful partnership working can result in powerful gains in terms of strengthening leadership, motivating staff and promoting continuing professional development. Many education-alists, including Hoghughi (1999) and Daniels *et al.* (2003), are largely of the same opinion that partnerships, particularly those associated with parents, help to:

- improve children's educational performance;
- extend the contexts for learning and development;
- enhance children's self esteem and behaviour;
- improve parent–child relationships; and
- develop positive attitudes in parents towards schools and a better understanding of the schooling process (see Parker-Jenkins *et al.* 2007: 79).

But what is meant by the term 'partnership'? It is likely that you will have your own ideas with regard to this concept and you are encouraged to keep these in mind when engaging with this chapter. However, for clarification purposes, we define partnerships as effective links between two or more bodies which work towards a designated goal. A behavioural partnership would include people or organizations collaborating to ensure standards of children's behaviour are not only maintained but also improved. Whilst most academic literature is keen to examine partnerships largely within the context of parents and the local community, we feel it is important to initially consider those partnerships which are essentially in-house and are attributed to colleagues with whom you will have daily contact.

ACTIVITY

Consider who, among those you come into contact with during a typical school day, you are able to collaborate with to support effective behaviour management in the classroom. Make a list of these people and then compare your responses to the details below.

It is likely you will have identified some or all of the following:

- Head teacher
- Learning mentors or learning support practitioners
- Deputy head teacher
- Midday supervisors
- Teaching assistants
- Other teachers
- Assistant head teacher
- Kitchen staff
- Advanced skills teachers
- Higher level teaching assistants
- Students
- Family learning practitioners
- Cleaning staff
- Special educational needs co-ordinators
- Behaviour co-ordinators
- Caretaker
- Lead behaviour professionals

It is possible to work in partnership with *all* of these different members of staff, even though many of them will have little direct contact with the children you work with. Ways in which these partnerships may operate include the following:

- Kitchen staff – maintaining high expectations of children by promoting the use of good manners in the dinner hall, modelling positive social conventions by warmly greeting children.
- Students – encouraging them to adopt aspects of the school policy on behaviour management as part of their day-to-day practice – for example, using verbal praise generously to motivate and reward children for their efforts and achievements.
- Midday supervisors – implementing strategies developed in collaboration with the class teacher to manage behaviours in the dining hall, consistently referring back to the school rules when dealing with difficulties, having a shared philosophy of behaviour management with the school, such as 'look for the good'.
- Assistant head teacher – using whole-school management systems with efficiency and effectiveness, awareness of strategies used by different classes/key stages, adopting a firm but fair approach throughout the entire school.
- Caretaker – modelling positive behaviours when welcoming children, parents and cleaning staff into the school, having high expectations of children when interacting with them, following procedures by reporting behavioural issues in a professional and non-judgemental manner to relevant practitioners.

One of the most important partnerships we can have in school is with our teaching assistants – if you are fortunate enough to work with one, that is. By working closely together, you are in a better position to establish a shared understanding of effective behaviour management in the classroom, developing and deploying strategies, approaches and ideas in collaboration and with consistency, which is recognized by most educationalists and practitioners as the most important aspect of effective behaviour management. Managing behaviour can become a real battle if you say and do one thing and your teaching assistant says and does another – having joined-up thinking is of real benefit to any partnership. Teaching assistants can prove to be invaluable at times, particularly when you are in need of time out or breathing space from children with behavioural difficulties. Directing the child to another adult allows you to personally reflect on your actions to date, and to reconsider the approach and strategies you intend to use to try and manage the behaviour being exhibited. By doing this you ensure that your next contact with the child is positive, balanced and amicable.

The important thing to remember, however, is that because this is a partnership you should be in a position to take on this role for your teaching assistant if they are having difficulties with a child. Sometimes parents/carers can become a little distant and appear reticent to speak with you because of being told that their child is unfortunately badly behaved, so teaching assistants may act as a useful go-between, ensuring that avenues for communication remain open. For this kind of partnership to exist with your teaching assistant it is important that you:

- have an open and honest working relationship with each other;
- allow your teaching assistant to contribute to discussions, and ensure you listen with care and consideration to what is said by them;
- ensure your teaching assistant is part of the decision-making process and is happy with the decisions made;
- keep your teaching assistant up to date with any developments;
- ask your teaching assistant to regularly update you with how things are going, not only from the child's perspective but from the assistant's personal perspective as well.

Many of the suggestions offered above are useful in helping to build and maintain partnerships with parents, which we will now examine in more detail.

Parental partnerships

Parental involvement continues to be identified by reports and research as one of the key variables in effective school improvement (Chabourdy *et al.* 2001, cited in Fitzgerald 2004). There are a number of ways in which schools are working to promote parental involvement in their individual settings. Among these strategies are the following:

- encouraging parents to come into school as parent helpers;
- holding parents' open days;
- providing community mother and toddler groups;
- allowing parents to contribute to the records kept on their child;
- employing parents as midday supervisors or teaching assistants;
- putting on parent workshops which model learning and teaching processes – for example, how children learn to read;
- actively involving parents in the work of the school's parent friend association;
- encouraging parents to be governors of the school;
- planning homework for children to do with their parents (OFSTED 1999b; Beveridge 2005).

We recognize that many children in our classrooms are looked after by carers and that partnerships with carers are just as important. For clarification purposes, we use the term 'parent' in this chapter to encompass both parents and carers.

REFLECTION

What do you think the benefits of these strategies are, particularly with regard to managing and improving standards of behaviour in school? Compare your thoughts with others.

A number of the strategies suggested above do have the potential to make a real difference to children's behaviour in school:

Strategy	Outcome
Encouraging parents to be governors of the school	Parents are able to review and comment on the content of behaviour policies in the school
Holding parents' open days	Parents are able to see behaviour management 'in action' in their child's class and in classes throughout the school
Providing community mother and toddler groups	Parents can observe strategies being used by practitioners and other parents to manage children's behaviour and adopt these as their own
Encouraging parents to come into school as helpers	Parents will learn management strategies from the teacher through them being modelled in both whole-class and group-work situations. They will be then in a better position to use these in the home environment

We should remember that parents ultimately have a responsibility for managing the behaviour of their children, and so there should be an *expectation* that parents will work with teachers to manage behaviour difficulties. There are, however, some parents who will be reluctant to engage in this kind of activity, and you need to be aware of the potential reasons why this may be the case. Read the following scenario and draw out different factors which highlight why some parents may not work in partnership with schools.

SCENARIO

After Jake had exhibited poor behaviour for a number of weeks, Mr Johnson, the Year 6 class teacher, invited the child's mother and father into school to establish a plan of action. Mr Johnson had sent a number of letters home with Jake, but had not received any reply. Eventually Mr Johnson decided to phone Jake's home and managed to arrange a meeting with Jake's mother. Jake's father did not attend the meeting as he was working – Jake's mother explained that she had received all of the letters but they had used 'too many big words' for her to understand, which made her feel 'thick'. Coupled with the arrival of a new baby, and issues with money and housing, Jake's mother had had little time to sort things out. She was reluctant to come into the school, saying that she hated classrooms after her own time at school, and was deeply suspicious of Mr Johnson as he discussed some of the behaviours Jake had been exhibiting.

It is relatively easy to formulate a number of strategies and recommendations which would pre-empt issues like those above from developing:

- Avoid contacting parents after a number of weeks of poor behaviour – try to 'nip it in the bud early on'.
- Use alternatives to letters to communicate with parents – use the telephone, e-mail, messages in reading records, text messages and/or verbal reminders via the child.
- Ensure any written communication with parents conveys the message in a simple and straightforward manner. Avoid educational jargon wherever possible to protect parents' self-esteem.
- Appreciate that parents lead busy lives and it may be necessary to rearrange meetings – be flexible with dates and times you set.
- Empathize with parents who may have had negative experiences in the classroom when they were children.

Another strategy worth considering is to ensure that you let parents know you want to work in partnership with them to address the difficulties being experienced in school, and potentially at home: 'links with parents are most successful when parents are seen as partners rather than being blamed for the poor behaviour of their children' (OFSTED 2005: 18). This means that teachers need to work closely with parents so that they can:

- share ideas and information with each other in a collaborative manner;
- establish 'two-way' forms of communication to maintain healthy and purposeful dialogue about children's behaviour;
- adopt a 'no-blame' approach to managing their child's behaviour;
- regularly assess the effectiveness of their actions and adapt practice accordingly;
- develop an honest and open relationship with parents.

Dix (2007: 96) advocates the idea of teachers trying to 'ask for advice and support' rather than telling parents what you want them to do. The thinking behind this is that it will open up a purposeful dialogue and empower the parents, making them feel as if they are positively contributing to proceedings. You should ensure that decisions are made in agreement with the parents and that they are clear as to what is expected of them, knowing what they can do if they encounter any difficulties. By setting and keeping to review dates and regularly updating parents with feedback as to how things are progressing in school, it is likely that issues will be dealt with effectively and quickly. Miller *et al.* (2005) provide some useful suggestions, which we hope, will be of value to you:

- Give time to those parents who need it – this may be before or after school or even during teaching time.
- Offer support and advice as and when you can, not only with regard to educational issues but also to personal, social and health concerns.

- Be sympathetic to parents' needs.
- Work to build trust – if you say you intend do something you must follow it through and complete it to the best of your ability.

Another form of parental involvement worth mentioning relates to many schools actively encouraging parents to come and work as volunteers in school, the benefits of which cannot be underestimated (DfES 2003a; Smit *et al.* 2002). However, a number of schools have found this has not had as positive an impact on children's behaviour as expected.

CASE STUDY

In the South-West of England a primary school wanted to engage more parents in children's learning and so invited them into school to work in their children's classrooms, supporting groups with their activities. It was quickly noted that children's behaviour throughout the school began to deteriorate, and staff were keen to establish why this was the case. Eventually the problem was found to be that many parents were only willing to work with their own child, and this usually resulted in their child 'playing up'. It was also discovered that parents were not knowledgeable about the behaviour policy of the school and so were not aware of the behaviours they should expect/not expect from the children. Many pupils saw the parents coming in as 'an easy touch' and began to display inappropriate forms of behaviour which they would not have been able to get away with otherwise – making silly noises, engaging in excessive idle chatter and producing work of a substandard level. Many parents were at a loss as to how to manage these behaviours, either accepting them as the norm or ignoring them.

Class teachers noticed how some parents lacked confidence with some of the subject-matter being taught, particularly that related to literacy and numeracy, and found parents were either teaching the children incorrectly or were not teaching them at all, 'childminding' them, as one class teacher put it, whilst encouraging their group to make sure their work was neat. This frustrated some of the pupils, particularly those in upper Key Stage 2, as they either made little progress in lessons or received few positive marks or comments from the class teacher when their work was marked.

As a result, the school had to quickly reassess the way in which it had approached the idea of parental involvement in the classroom and put into place strategies to manage the issues which had resulted from this approach.

What do you think the school did wrong which resulted in the issues surrounding children's behaviour in the classroom? What would you have done to prevent these issues from occurring in the school? We reflected on this scenario ourselves and came up with the following ideas:

- Parents need to appreciate that they are there to support individuals and groups of children, not just their own child. Many schools are now working to ensure this does not become an issue by stipulating in their parental involvement policy that parents are not allowed to work in classrooms in which their own children are taught.
- Parents need to be planned for carefully by the class teacher, ideally playing to their strengths and interests.
- Parents need to be inducted into the school, having time to read the behaviour policy in an appropriate format, whilst observing the teacher working with the class so that they can see management strategies being put in place. They then should be in a better position to identify behaviours which are expected of the children they work with.
- Parents need to have a clear idea of what they are to do with the children they support *prior* to actually engaging with the task – they need to have time to ask any questions and work with the teacher so that they appreciate some of the difficulties children may have with the work and what support they are able to give them.
- Class teachers need to work with their class to promote positive and respectful behaviours towards parent helpers, stressing how privileged they are to be working with them. PSHCE and circle time opportunities are ideal for this.
- Class teachers need to give parents feedback on how they are doing, offering them generous praise and small pointers so that they are able to support the children to the very best of their ability.

NOTE

All schools across Britain face a greater challenge in encouraging parental involvement due the need for Criminal Records Bureau (CRB) checks to be conducted on those wishing to work with children or other vulnerable members of society. Whilst these are designed to protect youngsters, parents may perceive the complicated paperwork, designated fees and lengthy amount of time required to process the application as an unnecessary burden just to work with children for an afternoon a week. Details and guidelines relating to these CRB checks can be found on http://www.crb.gov.uk.

EXTENDING YOUR LEARNING

You are encouraged to read the following publications to extend your knowledge and understanding linked to effective practice involving parents in children's education:

Desforges, D. and Abouchaar, A. (2003) *The Impact of Parental Involvement, Parental Support and Family Education on Pupil Achievement and Adjustment: A Literature Review*, Research Report RR433. London: DfES.
Hallam, S., Rogers, L. and Shaw, J. (2004) *Improving Children's Behaviour and Attendance through the Use of Parenting Programmes: An Examination of Good Practice*, Research Report 585. London: DfES.
Moran, P. and Ghate, D. (2004) *What Works in Parenting Support*. London: DfES.

When considering partnerships it is recommended that you reflect on the impact that partnerships with members of the local community can have on children's behaviour.

Partnerships with the local community

There is a known metaphor which refers to the child as a 'three-legged stool' supported by the school, home and the community (Dix 2007). This remains prevalent in today's society as behaviour management should ideally be supported by those who come into contact with the child. Links with the community tend to be specific to each individual area but links with groups might include:

- Places of worship
- The media – local radio, television and the press
- The police
- Charities and support organizations
- Sports clubs
- Local shops and businesses
- Neighbours, family members and friends
- Museums and galleries
- Sports centres
- Music, dance and drama groups

The use of music, dance and drama has already been discussed in the previous chapter, whilst the use of sports centres and clubs helps to put thinking and practice behind physical activity (see Chapter 6) into a new and valuable context. Let us then consider the potential of partnerships with the police.

The police

In 2002 the DfES published the *School Police Protocol* which set out guidelines and gave advice to help schools build more effective links and relationships with local police forces.

QUESTIONS

- Why do you think the DfES saw it as being important for schools to build these effective links and relationships?
- How can local constabularies potentially help to manage children's behaviour in schools?

Many of you will be aware of the police coming into schools to talk to the children about a number of topics, including road safety, the dangers of taking drugs, carrying weapons, stranger danger, being safe around fireworks and crime in general. Whilst this is clearly of benefit, it is important to remember that the police are not trained teachers and many in the past have been unaware of effective ways to deliver material to children whilst holding their attention. We can recall on occasion trying to manage halls full of inattentive, restless and fidgety children in school as presentations were given by police officers who simply talked at the children for twenty-five minutes. However, through role-play scenarios, cartoon characters, songs, puppets, catchphrases, work cards, problem-solving opportunities and interactive games, the police are now more able to get hard-hitting messages across to the children in age-appropriate and effective ways.

NOTE

The police are largely able to address issues pertinent to either the school itself or the local community as and when they occur. This ensures that the service provided remains responsive to current needs and demand.

As part of Safer School Partnerships (see Metropolitan Police 2008) police forces have been increasingly involved in working collaboratively with head teachers, governors, local authorities and teachers to address high levels of crime and antisocial behaviour committed in and around schools by and against young people. By providing selected secondary schools with a dedicated school beat (or liaison) officer, the police are able to ensure that provision is given to the school's feeder primary schools. The role of this officer is to work in partnership with children, young people, school staff across this 'family' of schools, and the wider community to:

- jointly identify and work with those children and young people identified as being at high risk of victimization, offending and social exclusion;
- prevent and reduce crime, antisocial behaviour and related incidents in and around the school; and

- tackle bullying and violence experienced by pupils and staff, truancy and exclusion, damage to school buildings and drug-related incidents.

The officer is also in a position to enable pupils to move through the transition phase from primary to secondary schools without being victimized, whilst supporting the introduction of conflict resolution techniques, such as restorative justice, into the school environment. Are you aware of school beat officers in your area? How might they be able to help you in your setting?

EXTENDING YOUR LEARNING

For information on restorative justice, see Braithwaite, J. (2004) Youth Development Circles, in J. Wearmouth, R.C. Richmond, T. Glynn and M. Berryman (eds) *Understanding Pupil Behaviour in Schools: A Diversity of Approaches*. London: David Fulton.

Local shops and businesses

All children will live in the vicinity of local shops and businesses and are likely to use these as part of their day-to-day life. These may include corner shops, supermarkets, hairdressers, florists, banks, childcare facilities, video stores, opticians, Chinese take-aways, and fish and chip shops. All of these shops and businesses have the potential of influencing positive behaviours in children by working in partnership with local schools. But many of you may be sceptical about the potential impact that, for example, a video store may have on children's behaviour, so let us examine this in a little more detail.

Many video stores stock films, computer games, television boxed sets, cartoons, and foods and drinks, all of which children will be eager to get their hands on. All of these have the potential to impact on the behaviour of children:

- Films with 12, 12A, 15 or 18 ratings are likely to contain scenes of violence which children may try to imitate.
- Many computer games now have classification ratings due to their violent or adult content.
- Television boxed sets may contain inappropriate language which children may attempt to integrate into their own.
- Children enjoy fast and furious cartoons, which may result in them becoming hyperactive and unruly.
- Foods containing additives and drinks with high sugar levels may cause children's behaviour to become undesirable.

Obviously staff who work at the stores have a duty to ensure children are not allowed to hire or purchase items which are not appropriate for them, and this supports local schools by ensuring these items do not fall into the wrong hands. However, as the case study below shows, there are times when video stores may need the support of schools.

CASE STUDY

The proprietor of a local video store in Kent contacted a local primary school to complain about the way in which his staff were being spoken to by children who attended the school. He made the head teacher aware of how children were being blatantly rude, deliberately knocking DVD cases and boxes off the shelves, and were unnecessarily loud and obnoxious to other customers in the store. Incidences of theft and 'mud pies' being thrown at the windows of the shop eventually forced the proprietor to telephone the school.

The head teacher promptly held a meeting with the proprietor and they discussed some approaches and strategies which they could collaboratively use with the children. A day later the head teacher held a whole-school assembly in which he talked about the behaviours he expected to see in the school, namely those associated with politeness, respect for others' belongings and treating others appropriately. Drawing these points together he linked them to the rules of the school and then turned to the children and said: 'If you can do it in our school then you can do it in our community!'

He made the school aware of the behaviours exhibited by 'certain children' at the video store and stated that he would be taking a 'zero tolerance' stance on any further incidences which occurred there, expressing his disappointment in a few who had tarnished the good name of the school. Subdued, the school was asked to take stock of what the head teacher had said during playtime.

The proprietor of the store immediately noticed a marked difference in the children's behaviour. This was reinforced by the head teacher's recommendation to create a sign to be put in the shop window stating that only two children would be allowed in the store at any one time unless accompanied by an adult. The store created a small number of displayed 'expectations' of customers which stressed the importance of staff being spoken to politely, items being returned to the shelves for others to view, and of customers moderating the volume of their voice for the benefit of others.

As a way of thanking the school, the video store allowed the school to borrow a number of appropriate new releases for the last Friday afternoon before the end of each term.

By reinforcing rules and expectations in both verbal and written form, the head teacher and the proprietor of the video store were able to work together to ensure a speedy and effective resolution to the issues which were presented. Interestingly, the notion of zero tolerance is usually a response evoked as a result of incidences of bullying. The concept originates from the theory of James Q. Wilson (see Rigby 2004) which highlights how allowing small 'crimes' to pass unpunished encourages contempt for the law in larger matters. The thinking is that by stamping on the minor behaviours seen in school we are simultaneously reducing the likelihood of more severe behaviours occurring in society. Whilst the case study above goes some way to putting this theory into effective practice, you should be aware of how zero tolerance policies can appear to be undiscriminating, not only in their execution but also in conception and intention. For an interesting discussion of this you are recommended to take a look at http://www.abanet.org/crimjust/juvjus/zerotolreport.html.

Religious groups

It would be possible to write an entire book about the infinite ways in which different religions and their beliefs have a positive impact on the behaviour of children and adults who embrace them. However, for the purposes of this book, it is sufficient to highlight the fact that the world faiths have a shared understanding when it comes to advocating:

- honesty and truth;
- integrity;
- caring for one's own family and friends;
- honour;
- respect;
- love.

Many of the above are dispositions, which effectively promote positive behaviours in our children, and so it is important for all teachers to provide opportunities for children to develop these through spiritual, moral, social and cultural activities (see http://www.smsc.org.uk, with particular reference to the 'library' section). One of the ways this can be achieved is through working with religious groups. Ways in which this may be achieved include:

- local priests and nuns taking assemblies during which they tell children religious stories that advocate positive behaviours;
- religious theatre groups delivering plays based on stories from religious texts – the Good Samaritan from the Bible;
- members of a particular faith teaching children authentic hymns and chants;
- local clergy members working with teachers to deliver information linked to religious education units of work to small groups or the whole class;
- children making visits to local places of worship, observing acts of worship where appropriate.

All of these strategies provide opportunities for children to consider the importance of right and wrong, the consequences of their actions, and will encourage them to display appropriate forms of behaviour, all of which will impact on the quality of behaviour in school. Knowing which religious groups are in your local area and locating useful contact details is the first step to initiating partnerships with them – many have designated people to support this kind of work. Most religious groups undertake this work with no costs attached, but it is usually recommended that voluntary contributions are made by the school as a way of thanking them for their continued efforts and support. This kind of practice is also useful when working with museums and galleries.

Museums and galleries

Partnerships with museums and galleries are a useful way in which the curriculum, particularly history and art and design, can come alive for children and learning can be put into a vibrant and stimulating context. Many of these partnerships have come about due to the rise in work being undertaken with Creative Partnerships (see http:// www.creative-partnerships.com). However, taking children out of the safety of the 'four walls of the classroom' inevitably brings with it behavioural difficulties as some children become overly excited, silly and difficult to control. Teachers are becoming increasingly reluctant to take children on trips due to issues like these, coupled with considerations linked to costs, risk assessments and the general stress of the day. To pre-empt some of these behavioural issues from occurring, museums and galleries have collaborated with schools to develop agreed 'codes of behaviour', which are shared with teachers and children prior to and during their visits. An example of one of these codes of behaviour is presented below:

> Code of Behaviour at the Museum
> - Teachers and adult helpers are responsible for supervising the behaviour of their group at all times.
> - Ensure you have an appropriate ratio of adults to children to supervise your group. We recommend one adult per five children for KS1 and younger, and one adult per six children for KS2 and older.
> - Children should be encouraged to use our hands-on exhibits safely. Teachers and parent helpers must intervene if they see a child using an object in a dangerous or destructive manner.
> - For their own safety, children should be stopped from running in the galleries.
> - After use, children are expected to put hands-on exhibits back in their proper place for other visitors to enjoy.
> - Report any damage to a member of staff at the Information Desk.
> - Do not allow children to climb on Museum displays or furniture.
> (Museum of Childhood 2008)

Whilst this is a supportive measure, it is useful to remember that museums and galleries have a responsibility themselves to prevent behavioural difficulties when the children are actually on site. Many behavioural incidents are a result of:

- poor welcoming of classes into the setting by staff members;
- unstimulating or inappropriate delivery of information by guides who do not pitch the subject content at the right level for children to understand;

- lack of understanding of museum and gallery staff about engagement with the children;
- not enough artefacts for children to handle at the same time, thus creating long queues of restless children;
- few interactive exhibits to engage the children; and
- poor toilet facilities.

QUESTIONS

- How might museums and galleries be able to address some of these considerations so as to prevent behavioural difficulties?
- Are there any other considerations you can think of which may have an adverse effect on children's behaviour in either museums or galleries?

With these kinds of issues to contend with, it is valuable to build partnerships with museums and galleries to ensure that:

- both the school and museum/gallery know their specific role during the visit;
- the exhibitions presented will be stimulating for the children to view and engage with;
- there is plenty for the children to do – drawing, problem-solving, observing, playing with artefacts, exploring and investigating, writing, role-play opportunities, dressing up, being able to ask questions;
- guides and support staff understand how children learn, can relate to them on an appropriate level and are keen to interact with them;
- information is provided in child-friendly language;
- enough materials, both consumable and non-consumable, are available and are on hand for the children to access as and when necessary;
- access to child-friendly toilet facilities is made available throughout the visit.

Whilst it is hoped that this section on working with the local community has made you appreciate the benefits of partnership work, it is essential that we take a moment to consider the impact that the *Every Child Matters* agenda has had on partnerships and the benefits this will bring, particularly to improving children's behaviour.

Every Child Matters and partnerships

The publication of *Every Child Matters: Change for Children* (DfES 2004) brought the notion of effective partnerships to the forefront of people's minds. The government felt that the 'organisations involved with providing services to children – from hospitals and schools, to police and voluntary groups – need to team up in new ways, sharing information and working together, to protect children and young people from harm and help them achieve what they want in life'. Through this integrated way of working it has been necessary for what is now known as the DCSF to produce a multitude of publications, materials and toolkits to give effective support to practitioners who deliver a range of services for children and young people.

> ### EXTENDING YOUR LEARNING
>
> Visit http://www.everychildmatters.gov.uk, paying particular attention to the section entitled 'Delivering Services'. Take time to search through the materials in this section, considering how information, advice and ideas may directly impact on your practice in the classroom linked to effective behaviour management.
>
> Alternatively, take a look at the two case studies at www.dfes.gov.uk/ behaviourimprovement/multi-agency/index.cfm which show multi-agency work in action in Bristol and Wolverhampton.

Raising awareness of multi-agency work is an important part of this chapter as it is likely that you will work with a variety of practitioners to support children's behaviour in your classroom. Being aware of who these people actually are is not enough; you, as the teacher, need to be aware of what services they are able to provide and consider ways in which you can work in partnership so there are clear benefits for you, them and the children the support is designed for. Let us begin by examining the valuable work of educational psychologists.

Educational psychologists

Educational psychologists are largely concerned with helping children who are experiencing problems within an educational setting, with the aim of enhancing their learning. Problems may include learning difficulties and social or emotional problems. They primarily work with individual children or small groups, providing advice for teachers, parents and other professionals who work with the child. For children with behavioural difficulties they are a useful source of assessment, support, training, guidance and knowledge. But where can teachers go to seek the services of educational psychologists to support their practice? It is recommended that you work to establish whether they are employed in your area by the local authority as part of the educational psychology service, are self-employed and work as independent consultants for parents, or work in social services departments or voluntary agencies.

Being aware of the duties of educational psychologists is important as many of you engaging with this text may not know or understand the essential roles they undertake. These are quite varied but generally include the following:

- Focusing on early problem identification and early intervention
- Undertaking therapeutic work with children and young people and their parents or carers

- Assisting schools with the development of SEN policies so that the performance of the whole school is enhanced
- Engaging in action research to promote increased teacher knowledge of good practice in the areas of inclusion and raised achievement
- Engaging in projects to raise achievement and improve provision for pupils with emotional and behavioural difficulties
- Helping to develop knowledge and skills for teachers, learning support assistants and governors
- Working in multi-agency contexts with health, social services, voluntary services and other agencies
- Supporting parents as 'key partners'.

(http://www.everychildmatters.gov.uk/ete/agencies/psychology)

REFLECT

Reflect on the roles identified above and consider how each one influences or has an impact on children's behaviour in schools.

Bringing in the expertise of educational psychologists is useful, especially when a teacher has difficulty in successfully engaging with *any* of the three steps linked to the 'be clear' approach to effective behaviour management (see Figure 1 in Chapter 3).

CASE STUDY

A Year 5 teacher in an inner-city primary school in Manchester was struggling to manage the behaviour of a particular boy, and even though she had twenty years of teaching experience she was unable to establish what was wrong with him. Seeking the support of an educational psychologist proved to be invaluable as he was able to undertake a mixture of different assessments of the child, including observations (both in the classroom and on the playground), discussions with the parents, teachers and teaching assistants, and standardized psychometric tests and measures. From the wealth of information generated, the educational psychologist was quickly able to establish that the child had Asperger's syndrome.

Whilst the work of educational psychologists has been strongly advocated it is important to recognize that many do not necessarily work alone, but collaborate with other professionals from the fields of health, social care and education to form behaviour and education support teams (BESTs).

Behaviour and education support teams

The aim of a BEST is to promote emotional well-being, positive behaviour and school attendance by identifying and supporting those with, or who are at risk of developing, emotional and behavioural problems. BESTs work with children and young people aged 5–18, their families and schools to intervene early and prevent problems developing further. They are strategically placed in targeted primary and secondary schools, and in the community, alongside a range of other support structures and services. Successful BESTs bring together the skills, perspectives and experience of a range of practitioners, forming an effective multi-disciplinary team. A BEST contains a mixture of staff members, who between them have a complementary mix of education, social care and health skills in order to meet the multi-faceted needs of children, young people and their parents. A typical team may include:

- Behaviour support staff
- Clinical psychologists
- Education welfare officers
- Educational psychologists
- Health visitors
- Primary mental health workers
- School nurses
- Social workers/family workers

REFLECT

- Do you know of a BEST in your local area?
- How might you be able to make contact with a BEST?
- How might they be able to support you with difficulties you might be experiencing in your school at present?

Other BEST collaborators include speech and language therapists, whose work is of great value when managing children's behaviour.

Speech and language therapists

Speech and language therapists assess and treat speech, language and communication problems in people of all ages in different settings to enable them to communicate to the best of their ability. They also work with parents/carers and others to assess if a child has eating and drinking difficulties. There is strong research (see http://www.speechtherapy. co.uk) to support the idea that communication skills are crucial for intellectual, educational, social and emotional development, and this is why speech and language therapists work with children and young people who have problems with understanding, expressing themselves and using communication to socialize appropriately. It is likely that children with these difficulties will become increasingly frustrated and anxious with their inability to communicate effectively, and will show this in inappropriate forms of behaviour including punching, kicking and biting. By working with speech and language therapists, teachers are likely to reduce the likelihood of these behaviours occurring.

NOTE

Anyone can refer children to speech and language therapy. However, if this person is someone other than the child's parents, then the referral must always be made with the parents' consent.

Some teachers, however, remain unclear about the different aspects of what speech and language therapists actually do. The activity below is designed to make you independently aware of their different roles.

ACTIVITY

Speech and language therapists engage in five main activities:

- referral;
- assessment;
- reporting;
- interventions; and
- discharge.

Carry out some personal research into the roles and responsibilities of speech and language therapists to gain an appreciation of what each role entails and how this can used to support children with behavioural difficulties in school. How do they compare to the work of educational psychologists?

Take a moment to consider if there are any children with whom you work who would benefit from speech and language therapy. Do these children exhibit poor behaviour as a result of their difficulties with speech and language? Prime responsibility for the provision of speech and language therapy services to children has rested with the National Health Service (NHS) since 1974, and so you are reminded to contact your local health services when trying to refer children for speech and language support. The process of referring a child will largely involve a number of telephone calls, discussions with specific individuals, filling in forms and completing other paperwork. You are encouraged to locate copies of forms you will need so that you are at least aware of the kind of information you will need to gather. Effective record keeping and filing systems, both paper and electronic, will go some way to managing this process appropriately. This kind of practice is also useful when referring children to education welfare officers.

Education welfare officers

Education welfare officers (also known as education social workers) support local authorities in checking that parents ensure their children of compulsory school age (5–16) attend school regularly. Many children with poor attendance are likely to have behavioural difficulties as they are not well accustomed to the rules and regulations of the school, being unaware of or easily forgetting the expectations of class teachers as a result of attending school for one or two days at a time. Education welfare officers work closely with schools and families to resolve attendance issues, arranging school and home visits as necessary.

As with the work of educational psychologists and speech and language therapists, children have to be formally referred to the education welfare service. However, it is important that schools are able to show that they have made, prior to this referral, some effort to address the non-attendance. But what strategies can be put in place to manage this?

THINK

- What might be some of the reasons why some children have a poor attendance at school?
- How might class teachers and schools be able to address effectively some of these issues to ensure better attendance of these children?

For support you are encouraged to look at the following websites:

- www.direct.gov.uk/en/Parents/Schoolslearninganddevelopment/Your ChildsWelfareAtSchool/DG_4016117
- www.dfes.gov.uk/schoolattendance/publications/index.cfm

Good links with education welfare officers ensure that any issues with attendance can be investigated and rectified. However, some children may have poor attendance due to poor health and so it is useful for teachers to be aware of the work of health visitors.

Health visitors

Health visitors are qualified nurses, experienced in child health, health promotion and health education. Their role is to help people of all age groups stay healthy and avoid illness. Health visitors are part of the NHS community health services and work closely with GPs, practice nurses, district nurses, school health nurses, midwives, social workers and schoolteachers. One of the great benefits of health visitors is that they are the most accessible health professionals in the community; you can get access to a health visitor through your GP surgery or health clinic. As they are there to help anyone, you do not need an appointment – many suggest you just phone and they will visit you at home if you wish. Many of you may be aware that every family with children under 5 years has a named health visitor. For practitioners in the early years this can be very advantageous as health visitors are able to offer continuing support, advising parents and teachers on children's:

- growth and development – behaviour;
- immunization programmes;
- safety in and outside the home;
- common illnesses;
- healthy eating;
- everyday difficulties, such as teething, sleeping, feeding, temper tantrums, where to find child minders, toddler groups, playgroups, day nurseries.

They can advise on appropriate childcare if you are returning to work. They can also put you in touch with other sources of help.

However, this raises an important question: how beneficial are health visitors for children in the primary classroom?

REFLECT

Taking each of the topics of discussion above in turn, consider how the work of health visitors may be of use to you in supporting children's behaviour in either Key Stage 1 or 2 classrooms. The first bullet point has been done for you as an example:

- Growth and development – health visitors may be able to establish whether aspects of the child's growth or development is having an adverse effect on their behaviour whilst being able to explain stages which children should go through in relation to their understanding and use of appropriate forms of behaviour.

Many of the partnerships mentioned have links in some way with local authorities, and we feel that even though this is the last 'partner' we shall highlight, they remain a very important partner with which to collaborate.

Local authorities

As you will most likely be working for a local authority, it is useful to remember that local authorities can offer teachers and schools varying degrees of support and guidance, particularly relating to managing and supporting children with behaviour difficulties. As local authorities operate in different ways, you are encouraged to make contact with key personnel in yours, as they will be in a better position to provide guidance, support and information relating to the following:

- procedures for referrals;
- teaching support;
- co-ordination of work of voluntary and statutory agencies;
- assessments of pupils;
- compilation of basic information and background details of families;
- access to behavioural support.

You should therefore:

- make contact with the authority through various means such as telephone, e-mail, letter;
- speak directly to key personnel – advisors and support staff;
- organize regular meetings with key personnel to support you – keep them informed of your progress and your needs;
- ensure you have their correct contact details – full names, times of availability and correct e-mail addresses, telephone numbers and postal address.

Support can also be sought through extended school provision and children's centres. Discussions with your local authority will also help develop your understanding of these important developments in education. However, at the time of writing, it is of our understanding that the work of local authorities nationally is to be downgraded and that school improvement officers or school improvement partners will undertake more of this work with a small number of schools.

Weighing up the pros and cons

No chapter on partnerships would be complete or balanced in content if we did not consider some of the cons of working in partnership with others – whilst we have advocated the use of partnerships to support the management of children's behaviour, there are many considerations which need to be addressed so partnerships can be effectively initiated, conducted and sustained. Many partnerships either become ineffective or break down due to:

- unreasonable expectations from different partners with regard to what each party can offer;
- lack of preparation;
- insufficient time given to developing action plans;
- one side of the partnership not pulling their weight and sharing out the workload evenly;
- misunderstandings causing tension between partners;
- funding either being cut or becoming unavailable;
- partners not being able to truly commit to the aims and actions of the partnership;
- individual partners having their own agenda which is not conducive to the main goal of the partnership;

- poor or lack of joined-up thinking;
- partners' lack of appreciation of the time and effort needed to make partnerships work;
- local or national targets interfering with specific targets set by the partnership;
- new colleagues being reluctant to embrace the work of others who set up the partnership;
- lack of a 'key person' overseeing all aspects of the partnership and therefore taking charge;
- sustainability issues.

Whilst we do not want to discourage you from considering using partnership work as an integral feature of your approach to behaviour management, it is necessary to reflect on the above and consider ways you could prevent these issues from occurring. Develop a plan of action if any of these points threaten to impact on the success of your partnership work. How could you ensure everyone pulls their weight? How would you dedicate time to preparing the work of the partnership – before, during or after school? How is it possible to make sure the thinking of the partnership is joined up? What other funding opportunities are available to you if a pot of money is depleted or suddenly disappears? Working alongside partners who are established and effective at leading and managing partnership work is valuable, as you will quickly get a sense of what works and what does not, thus allowing you to take good practice and adopt it as your own.

The most important aspect of any partnership work is that all partners must be 'singing from the same song sheet'. Dedicating time to developing a shared philosophy (see Chapter 1) and a set of aims is paramount so that everyone is working towards the same goal – to promote, develop and sustain good behaviour in all children with whom we have the privilege of coming into contact.

KEY POINTS

- Effective partnerships can ensure that children's behaviour is well supported, not only in school but also outside of it.
- Partnerships can be formed with many different people, not just with parents and the wider community.
- Partnerships must be based on collaboration, trust, honesty and team work to ensure they are sustained and effective.
- Teachers need to spend time making contact with their local authorities and health services to determine what services are available for them to use to support them with their practice in school.
- Appreciation of the different roles different agencies play is important to ensure services are used to their maximum potential.
- There are advantages and disadvantages to creating partnerships, and teachers should be mindful of these when they consider establishing one.

9 Looking forward

As we said at the outset of this book, there is no quick-fix cure for managing behaviour in the primary school. It takes time, patience and resilience to develop consistent and effective approaches to which pupils will respond. However, we do hope that you have found some useful information in this book to help you fight the battle against poor behaviour and come out a winner. We stated in Chapter 1 that all policies and practice related to behaviour management should not be allowed to become stagnant but be ever evolving and adaptable to match the needs of our pupils in school. The same of course could be said about us, whether we be teachers, students or support staff. Our understanding and response to the children we teach can be further improved and developed if we are proactive in our own continuing professional development. In order to do this:

- undertake a master's (MEd or MA) degree module in behaviour management to deepen your theoretical understanding in relation to practice;
- read a wide range of literature – journals, newspapers and academic research – to develop a variety of approaches and philosophies from a number of voices;
- attend conferences and training courses in the field of behaviour management;
- regularly review and reflect on your own practice in order to do the best for the children in your care;
- mentor a trainee teacher – through their good practice and their mistakes you will enhance your own knowledge of what does and does not work;
- take time in staff meetings to share good practice – collaborate with others to identify children in need of support and the best way to enable them to behave well in school.

Although it is essential to ensure that the well-being and social development of pupils are carefully considered, do not neglect your own well-being. Experience has shown that cream cakes are particularly good at lifting spirits and making you feel that little bit better and ready to face another day. Talk to staff members about your experiences in order to prevent your feelings from consuming you – a trouble shared is a trouble halved.

We know that most children will respond positively to a range of behaviour management strategies, which we have advocated in this book. We also know that there are those children who do not respond appropriately. These children are usually not to blame for their behaviour, but what is important is that you do not give up on them. Persevere, remain calm and communicate with parents and carers.

Remember you are a teacher, not a superhero. Although, on the other hand ...

References

Aromatherapy Council (2008) What is aromatherapy? http://www.aromatherapycouncil.co.uk/index_files/Page390.htm (accessed 9 June 2008).

BBC (1999) Education stress therapy for five-year-olds. www.news.bbc.co.uk/1/low/education/263993.stm (accessed 2 June 2008)

Beveridge, S. (2005) *Children, Families and Schools*. Abingdon: RoutledgeFalmer.

Bolton, G. and Heathcote, D. (1999) *So You Want to Use Role-Play?* Stoke-on-Trent: Trentham Books.

Boyatzis, R. and Burckle, M. (1999) *Psychometric Properties of the ECI*, Technical note. Boston, MA: Hay/McBer Group.

Braithwaite, J. (2004) Youth development circles, in J. Wearmouth, R.C. Richmond, T. Glynn and M. Berryman (eds) *Understanding Pupil Behaviour in Schools: A Diversity of Approaches*, London: David Fulton.

Brownhill, S. (2007) *Taking the Stress out of Bad Behaviour*. London: Continuum.

Brownhill, S., Shelton, F. and Gratton, C. (2006) *101 Essential Lists for Managing Behaviour in the Early Years*. London: Continuum.

Bruner, J. (1990) Folk pedagogies, in J. Leach and B. Moon (eds) *Learners and Pedagogy*. London: Sage.

BUPA (2007) Aromatherapy. http://hcd2.bupa.co.uk/fact_sheets/html/aromatherapy.html (accessed 9 June 2008).

Canter, L. and Canter, M. (1992) *Assertive Discipline – Positive Behavior for Today's Classroom*. Santa Monica, CA: Lee Canter and Associates.

Central Advisory Council for Education (1967) *Children and Their Primary Schools* ('Plowden Report'). London: HMSO.

Cohen, L., Manion, L. and Morrision, K. (2004), *A Guide to Teaching Practice*, 5th edition. London: RoutledgeFalmer.

Cole, T., Visser, J. and Upton, G. (1998) *Effective Schooling for Pupils with Emotional and Behavioural Difficulties*. London: David Fulton.

Cole, T., Visser, J. and Daniels, H. (2000) *The Framework for Intervention: Identifying and Promoting Effective Practice,* 2nd evaluation report for City of Birmingham LEA. University of Birmingham.

Cowie, H. and Wallace, P. (2000) *Peer Support in Action: From Bystander to Standing By*. London: Sage.

Cowley, S. (2006) *Getting the Buggers to Behave*, 3rd edition. London: Continuum.

Cremin, H. (2002) Pupils resolving disputes: successful peer mediation schemes share their secrets. *Support for Learning*, 17(3): 138–43.

Daniels, A. and Williams, H. (2000) Reducing the need for exclusions and statements of behaviour. *Educational Psychology in Practice*, 15(4): 221–7.

Daniels, H., Cole, T., Sellman, E., Sutton, J., Visser, J. with Bedward, J. (2003) *Study into Young People Permanently Excluded from School*, Research Report RR405. London: DfES.

DCSF (2007) Social and emotional aspects of learning: improving behaviour ... improving learning. http://www.standards.dfes.gov.uk/primary/publications/banda/seal (accessed 30 June 2008).

DCSF (2008) Partnership dividend. http://www.standards.dfes.gov.uk/sie/si/eips/partdividend/ (accessed 12 June 2008).

Desforges, D. and Abouchaar, A. (2003) *The Impact of Parental Involvement, Parental Support and Family Education on Pupil Achievement and Adjustment: A Literature Review*, Research Report RR433. London: DfES.

DfEE (2000) *Bullying – Don't Suffer in Silence. An Anti-bullying Pack for Schools.* London: DfEE.

DfES (2001) *Special Educational Needs Code of Practice.* London: DfES.

DfES (2002) *School Police Protocol.* London: DfES.

DfES (2003a) *Aiming High: Raising the Achievement of Minority Ethnic Pupils.* London: DfES.

DfES (2003b) *Every Child Matters*, London: DfES.

DfES (2003c) *Excellence and Enjoyment – A Strategy for Primary Schools.* Nottingham: DfES Publications.

DfES (2004) *Every Child Matters: Change for Children.* London: DfES.

Dix, P. (2007) *Taking Care of Behaviour: Practical Skills for Teachers.* Harlow: Pearson Longman.

Docking, J. and MacGarth, M. (2002) *Managing Behaviour in the Primary School,* 3rd edition. London: David Fulton.

Education and Skills Committee (2006) *The Schools White Paper: Higher Standards, Better Education for All.* London: The Stationary Office.

Eisenberg, N. (1986) *Altruistic Emotion, Cognition and Behaviour.* Hillsdale, NJ: Erlbaum.

Eisner, E.W. (1982) *Cognition and Curriculum. A Basis for Deciding What to Teach.* New York and London: Longman.

Elton, R. (1989), *Enquiry into Discipline in Schools.* London: HMSO.

Emmerson, E. (2001) *Challenging Behaviour. Analysis and Interventions in People with Learning Difficulties.* Cambridge: Cambridge University Press.

Epstein, C.F. (1998) *Deceptive Distinctions. Sex, Gender and the Social Order.* New Haven, CT: Yale University Press.

Evans, J.L., Myers, R.G. and Ilfeld, E.M. (2000) *Early Childhood Counts: A Programming Guide on Early Childhood Care for Development.* Washington, DC: World Bank Publications.

Fisher, R. (1995) *Teaching Children to Learn.* Cheltenham: Nelson Thornes.

Fisher, R. (2003) *Teaching Thinking.* London: Continuum.

Fitzgerald, D. (2004) *Parent Partnerships in the Early Years.* London: Continuum.

Food Commission (2003) Parents say that food does affect their children's behaviour. http://www.foodcomm.org.uk/parentsjury/add_3.htm (accessed 9 June 2008).

Gateshead Healthy Schools (n.d.) Citizenship in Gateshead schools. http://www.gate-sheadhealthyschools.org/documents/Young%20Sports%20Winners%20-Form%20.pdf (accessed 27 June 2008).

Gilligan, C. (1982) *In A Different Voice: Psychological Theory and Women's Development.* Cambridge, MA: Harvard University Press.

Glenn, A., Cousins, J. and Helps, A. (2004) *Behaviour in the Early Years.* London: David Fulton.

Greenhalgh, P. (1994) *Emotional Growth and Learning.* London: Routledge.

Hallam, S., Rogers, L. and Shaw, J. (2004), *Improving Children's Behaviour and Attendance through the Use of Parenting Programmes: An Examination of good Practice*, Research Report 585. London: DfES.

Hartshorne, H. and May, M.A. (1928) *Studies in the Nature of Character: I. Studies in Deceit.* New York: Macmillan.

Hayes, D. (2006) *Inspiring Primary Teaching: Insights Into Excellent Primary Practice.* Exeter: Learning Matters.

Healy, M.J. (2003) 'Don't talk bananas!' Positive management in the classroom. *Teaching Today,* 76: 23–6.

Henderson, M. (2007) Modern life: it's one step at a time, only much quicker. www.timesonline.co.uk/tol/news/uk/science/article1733967.ece (accessed 30 June 2008).

Hinds, D. (n.d.) Resources: Making good citizens. http://www.schoolzone.co.uk/resources/articles/Good_citizen.asp (accessed 30 May 2008).

Hoffman, M.L. (1978) Toward a theory of empathic arousal and development. In M.R. Lewis and L.A. Rosenblum (eds) *The Development of Affect*, pp. 227–56. New York: Plenum.

Hoffman, M.L. (1988) Cross-cultural differences in child-rearing goals, in R.A. LeVine, P.M. Miller and M.M. West (eds) *Parental Behaviour in Diverse Societies*. San-Francisco: Jossey-Bass.

Hoffman, M.L., and Salzstein, H.D. (1967) Parent discipline and the child's moral development. *Journal of Personality and Social Psychology*, 5: 45–7.

Hoghughi, M. (1999) Families hold the key. *Times Educational Supplement*, 12 February: 15.

Hook, P. and Vass, A. (2000) *Confident Classroom Leadership*. London: David Fulton.

Hook, P. and Vass, A. (2006) *Behaviour Management Pocketbook*. Alresford: Teachers Pocketbooks.

Hoy, D. (2004) Individual behaviour management plans and group support with infant age children: Troy's story, in B. Rogers (ed.) *How to Manage Children's Challenging Behaviour*. London: Paul Chapman.

Hutchinson, N. and Fannon, P. (2004) *Intervening Early: Promoting Positive Behaviour in Young Children*. London: David Fulton.

Imamoğlou, E.O. (1975) Children's awareness and usage of intention cues. *Child Development*, 46: 39–45.

James, A. (1993) *Childhood Identities: Social Relationships and the Self in Children's Experiences*. Edinburgh: Edinburgh University Press.

Kamen, T. (2003) *Teaching Assistant's Handbook*. London: Hodder and Stoughton.

Kassing, G. and Jay, D.M. (2003) *Dance Teaching Methods and Curriculum Design*. Leeds: Human Kinetics.

Kerr, M.M. and Nelson, C.M. (2006) *Strategies for Addressing Behavior Problems in the Classroom*, 5th edition. Upper Saddle River, NJ: Pearson Merrill Prentice Hall.

Kohlberg, L. (1969) Stage and sequence: The cognitive-developmental approach to socialization, in D.A. Goslin (ed.) *Handbook of Socialization Theory and Research*. Chicago, IL: Rand McNally.

Kyriacou, C. (2002) A humanistic view of discipline, in B. Rogers (*ed.*) *Teacher Leadership and Behaviour Management*. London: Paul Chapman.

Laming, H. (2003) *The Victoria Climbié Inquiry: Report*, Cm. 5730. Norwich: TSO.

Learning and Teaching Scotland (2007) Inclusive education – Beyond the classroom: Newbattle Community High School's 'holistic' approach. www.ltscotland.org.uk/ Inclusiveeducation/sharingpractice/schools/beyondtheclassroom.asp (accessed 9 June 2008).

MacKay, D. (2004) Guideline on the framework for staged intervention. Professional Practice Paper 5. http://www.midlothian.gov.uk/utilities/filedownload/filedownload.aspx?blob=8820 (accessed 9 June 2008).

Maines, B. (2003) *Reading Faces and Learning about Human Emotions*. London: Lucky Duck.

Matthews, B. (2006) *Engaging Education*. Maidenhead: Open University Press.

Mayall, B. (1999) Children in action at home and school, in M. Woodhead, D. Faulkner and K. Littleton (eds) *Making Sense of Social Development*. London: Routledge.

McCune, S.L., Stephens, D.E. and Lowe, M.E. (1999) *Barron's How to Prepare for the ExCET*, 2nd edition. Hauppage, NY: Barron's.

McSherry, J. (2001) *Challenging Behaviours in Mainstream Schools: Practical Strategies for Effective Intervention and Reintegration*. London: David Fulton.

Metropolitan Police (2008) Safer school partnerships. http://www.met.police.uk/saferschoolpartnerships (accessed 9 June 2008).

Miller, L., Cable, C. and Devereux, J. (2005) *Developing Early Years Practice*. London: David Fulton.

Mooney, P., Ryan, J.B., Uhing, B.M., Reid, R. and Epstein, M.H. (2005) A review of self-management interventions targeting academic outcomes for students with emotional and behaviour disorders. *Journal of Behavioural Education*, 14(3): 203–21. See also http://www.standards.dfes.gov.uk/research/themes/behaviour/selfmanagement/?view=printerfriendly (accessed 9 June 2008).

Moran, P. and Ghate, D. (2004) *What Works in Parenting Support*. London: DfES.

Mortimer, H. (2004) *Developing Individual Behaviour Plans in Early Years*. Tamworth: NASEN.

Museum of Childhood (2008) Code of behaviour. http://www.vam.ac.uk/moc/learning/ schools/code_of_behaviour/index.html.

National Heart Forum (2007) Signs of heart disease 2-year-olds. http://www.heartforum.org.uk (under construction).

North, I. (2005) Boy, 10, is youngest to get Asbo after reign of terror. *The Independent*, 10 February. http://www.findarticles.com/p/articles/mi_qn4158/is_20050210/ ai_n9503151 (accessed 9 June 2008).

Nucci, L. (2002) Moral development and moral education: An overview. http:// tigger.uic.edu/~lnucci/MoralEd/overview.html (accessed 9 June 2008).

OFSTED (1999a) *Principles into Practice: Effective Education of Pupils for EBD*. HMI Report. London: OFSTED.

OFSTED (1999b) *Raising the Attainment of Minority Ethnic Pupils: Schools and LEA Responses*. London: OFSTED.

OFSTED (2005) *Managing Challenging Behaviour*. London: OFSTED.

OFSTED (2006a) School information and self evaluation form – guidance for schools. http://www.ofsted.gov.uk/portal/site/Internet/menuitem.eace3f09a603f6d9-c3172a8a08a0c/?vgnextoid=01f786f8d80fe010VgnVCM1000003507640aRCRD (accessed 12 June 2008).

OFSTED (2006b) Alfreton Nursery School OFSTED report. http://www.ofsted.gov.uk/reports/pdf/?inspectionNumber=278941&providerCategoryID=2048&fileName=%5C%5Cschool%5C%5C112%5C%5Cs5_112485_20060907.pdf (accessed 12 June 2008).

OFSTED (2006c) *Improving Behaviour*. London: HMSO.

OFSTED (2007) *Managing Challenging Behaviour*. London: OFSTED.

Osborn, R. (2006) Bullying as a relationship problem. http://www.rtime.info/initiatives.htm (accessed 9 June 2008).

Parker-Jenkins, M., Hewitt, D., Brownhill, S. and Sanders, T. (2007) *Aiming High: Raising Attainment of Pupils from Culturally Diverse Backgrounds*. London: Paul Chapman.

Piaget, J. (1932) *The Moral Judgment of the Child*. London, Routledge & Kegan Paul.

Porter, L. (2007) *Behaviour in Schools: Theory and Practice for Teachers,* 2nd edition. Maidenhead: Open University Press.

Power, C., Higgins, A. and Kohlberg, L. (1989) *Lawrence Kohlberg's Approach to Moral Education*. New York: Columbia University Press.

QCA (1999) Schemes of work. Geography at Key Stages 1 and 2. Unit 5: Where in the world is Barnaby Bear? http://www.standards.dfes.gov.uk/schemes2/geography/geo5/?view=get (accessed 9 June 2008).

Reschke, K.L. (2005) Early moral development. Knowing children, Ohio State University Extension. http://fcs.osu.edu/hdfs/cw/bultins/moral-dev-grow-bw.pdf (accessed 10 June 2008).

Rest, J.R. (1983) Morality, in P.H. Mussen (ed.) *Handbook of Child Psychology, Vol 3: Cognitive Development*. New York: Wiley.

Rigby, K. (2004) What is to be done about bullying?, in J. Wearmouth, R.C. Richmond, and T. Glynn (eds) *Addressing Pupils' Behaviour: Responses at District, School and Individual Levels*. London: David Fulton.

Roffey, S. (2007) Taking account of student–teacher relationships. http://www.teachingexpertise.com/articles/taking-account-of-emotions-in-student-teacher-relationships-1734 (accessed 2 June 2008).

Rogers, B. (1997) *Cracking the Hard Class*. London: Paul Chapman.

Rogers, B. (2002), *Classroom Behaviour: A Practical Guide to Teaching, Behaviour Management and Colleague Support*, 2nd edition. London: Paul Chapman.

Rogers, B. (2007) *Behaviour Management: A Whole School Approach*, 2nd edition. London: Paul Chapman.

Saisan, J., de Benedictis, T., Barston, S. and Segal, R. (2007) Sleeping well. http://www.helpguide.org/life/sleeping.htm (accessed 12 June 2008).

Schaffer, R. (1996) *Social Development*. Oxford: Blackwell.

Sell, K. (2004) Measurement of difference or meaning (when working with challenging children), in B. Rogers (ed.) *How to Manage Children's Challenging Behaviour*. London: Paul Chapman.

Short, G. (1999) Children's grasp of controversial issues, in M. Woodhead, D. Faulkner and K. Littleton (eds) *Making Sense of Social Development*. London: Routledge.

Smit, F., Driessen, G. and Sleggers, P. (2002) Parental involvement and educational achievement. *British Education Research Journal*, 31(4): 509–32.

Smith-Autard, J. (2002) *The Art of Dance Education*. London: A. & C. Black.

Solomons, S. (2005) Using aromatherapy massage to increase shared attention behaviours in children with autistic spectrum disorders and severe learning difficulties. *British Journal of Special Education*, 32(3): 127–37.

TeacherNet (2007) The Social and Emotional Aspects of Learning (SEAL). http://www.teachernet.gov.uk/teachingandlearning/socialandpastoral/sebs1/seal/ (accessed 2 June 2008).

TeacherNet (2008) Healthy living to raise standards. www.teachernet.gov.uk/casestudies/casestudy.cfm?id=351 (accessed 9 June 2008).

TeacherNet (n.d.) A Summary of the Report's Main Findings. http://www.teachernet.gov.uk/supplyteachers/detail.cfm?&vid=4&cid=17&sid=107&ssid=4030501&opt=0 (accessed 27 June 2008).

Teaching Expertise (2006) Writing a behaviour policy. http://www.teachingexpertise.com/articles/writing-a-behaviour-policy-1253 (accessed 2 June 2008).

Tilstone, C. and Rose, R. (eds) (2003) *Strategies to Promote Inclusive Practice*. London: RoutledgeFalmer.

Visser, J. (2000) *Managing Behaviour in Schools*. London: David Fulton.

Wale-Carole, A. (2000) Kids get stressed too. *Safety Education*, 2000: 17–19.

Warne, A. (2003) Establishing peer mediation in a special school context. *Pastoral Care* (December): 27–33.

Weare, K. (2004) *Developing the Emotionally Literate School*. London: Paul Chapman.

Weber, K. (1982) *The Teacher Is the Key*. Milton Keynes: Open University Press.

Whitehead, A. (2006) How emotional intelligence affects behaviour. http://www.teachingexpertise.com/articles/how-emotional-intelligence-affects-behaviour-1438 (accessed 10 June 2008).

Womack, C. (2008) Aromatherapy. http://www.womack.org.uk/aroma.html (accessed 9 June 2008).

Index

UNDERSTANDING PHONICS AND THE TEACHING OF READING
A Critical Perspective

Kathy Goouch and Andrew Lambirth (eds)

Debates about the teaching of reading and particularly which phonics method teachers should use have been simmering for many years. This groundbreaking book offers critical perspectives on the teaching of reading and phonics, openly challenging contemporary policy in both England and the US.

As well as providing refreshing insights into how children encounter texts in the increasingly complex world of literacy, the book celebrates the complexity, pleasure and passion that are the foundations of becoming a successful reader. Each chapter explores in-depth the processes involved as children engage in reading, from their interactions with texts in the very earliest stages through to the primary phase. Drawing on both research and theory, the book also shows how some contemporary understandings of reading are based on over simplistic and rationalised ideas about the reading process.

A unique feature of this book is that it combines academic perspectives with the insights of parents and practitioners. The participation of those most closely involved with children complements the lively debate and contributions from researchers, providing a rich and inclusive range of ideas.

Understanding Phonics and the Teaching of Reading is a stimulating read for educational studies students, students of teaching and learning, policy makers, educational researchers and teachers.

Contents: *Contributors – Acknowledgements – Introduction – What is early childhood for? – Parents' voices: A conversation with parents of pre school children – Understanding educational discourse: Attending to multiple voices – The limits of science in the phonics debate – Teachers voices – To codify pedagogy or enrich learning? A Wengerian perspective on early literacy policy in England – Social class and the struggle to learn to read: Using Bernstein to understand the politics of the teaching of reading – Learning to read across languages: The role of phonics and synthetic phonics – Inquiry into meaning: A conversation – Revisiting reading for pleasure: Delight, desire and diversity.*

2008 216pp

978-0-335-22226-1 (Paperback) 978-0-335-22227-8 (Hardback)

SCIENCE FOR PRIMARY SCHOOL TEACHERS

Helena Gillespie and Rob Gillespie

- What do I need to know about science to teach children in primary school?
- How can I make my science teaching successful?
- How do children learn to investigate scientifically?
- What are the dos and don'ts of science teaching?

Written to support teachers who need to boost their science knowledge, this book covers science knowledge in sufficient breadth and depth to enable you to teach science effectively up to the end of Key Stage 2, as well as the core teaching and learning issues involved in the investigative process.

Whether you are a student or a fully qualified teacher, the book is designed to help you find what you need quickly. The introduction provides a guide to how to use the book, including a table which cross references the subject knowledge against the National Curriculum, the QCA Scheme of Work and Primary Science Topics. This enables you to use the book in different ways, depending on your individual requirements.

To ensure that teachers will be able to teach and respond to questions appropriately, the authors take science knowledge beyond what is required for Key Stage 2. This is important, as it helps to avoid over-simplifying concepts which can then cause misconceptions at Key Stage 3 and beyond. It also helps to broaden and develop the primary teacher's own knowledge.

Science for Primary School Teachers is a core text for teachers in training, and in professional development into the induction year and beyond.

Contents: *How to use this book – Acknowledgements – Section 1: Learning and teaching science: The investigative process – How children learn about science – Planning for teaching and learning: The process of scientific enquiry – Finding help with teaching and learning in science on the internet – Section 2: Subject knowledge for primary school teachers – Key concepts in science 2: Life processes and living things – Life processes – Humans and other animals – Green plants – Variation and classification – Living things and their environment – Key concepts in science 3: Materials and their properties – Grouping and classifying materials – Changing materials – Separating mixtures – Key Concepts in Science 4: Physical processes – Electricity – Forces and motion – Light and sound – The Earth and beyond – Glossary – Useful websites – Bibliography – Index.*

2007 216pp

978-0-335-22015-1 (Paperback) 978-0-335-22016-8 (Hardback)

DEVELOPING TEACHING SKILLS IN THE PRIMARY SCHOOL

Jane Johnston, John Halocha and Mark Chater

Teaching is a complex process which involves the development and utilization of subject knowledge and teaching skills. Containing reflective and practical skills, this book supports such development, focusing specifically on teaching skills, considering what they are, how they develop and how they differ between age and subject.

The book contains three sections Planning, Doing and Reviewing – which demonstrate effective classroom practice. It uses examples of practitioners at different stages of their professional development to link theory and practice, and includes discussions on contemporary issues in primary education, such as:

- Constructivist teaching and learning
- Thinking skills
- Creativity
- Teaching and learning styles
- Child-centred learning

The authors provide a critical analysis of the issues, practice and problems faced by primary school teachers, which is supported by reflective tasks throughout the book. Emphasizing the child as a partner in the learning process and highlighting the importance of teaching for child-centred learning, the book ultimately develops and strengthens the teacher's skills.

Developing Teaching Skills in the Primary School provides essential guidance and support to trainee, beginner and developing primary school teachers.

Contents: *Figures and pictures – Acknowledgements – Abbreviations – Developing teaching skills in the primary school – PART 1 Planning – Planning for creative teaching – Classroom organization – Planning for citizenship – Behaviour management – PART 2 Doing – Questioning – Differentiation – Using ICT in teaching – Supporting children in recording work – Developing investigative work / enquiry – PART 3 Reviewing – Assessment for learning – Target setting – Professional communication – Developing as a reflective practitioner – Index.*

2007 208pp

978-0-335-22096-0 (Paperback) 978-0-335-22095-3 (Hardback)

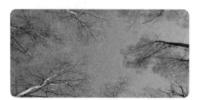